insight text guide

Virginia Lee

Brooklyn

Colm Tóibín

First published in 2013, reprinted in 2014, 2018, 2019, 2020.

Insight Publications Pty Ltd
3/350 Charman Road
Cheltenham VIC 3192
Australia
Tel: +61 3 8571 4950
Fax: +61 3 8571 0257
Email: books@insightpublications.com.au

www.insightpublications.com.au

National Library of Australia Cataloguing-in-Publication entry:
Lee, Virginia, author.
Colm Toibin's Brooklyn / Virginia Lee.
9781922150868 (paperback)
Insight text guide.
Includes bibliographical references.
For secondary school age.
Tóibín, Colm, 1955- . Brooklyn.
Tóibín, Colm, 1955- .— Criticism and interpretation.
Tóibín, Colm, 1955- , author. Brooklyn.
823.914

Other ISBNs:
9781925175042 (digital)
9781925175370 (bundle: print + digital)

Printed in Australia by Ligare

contents

CHARACTER MAP

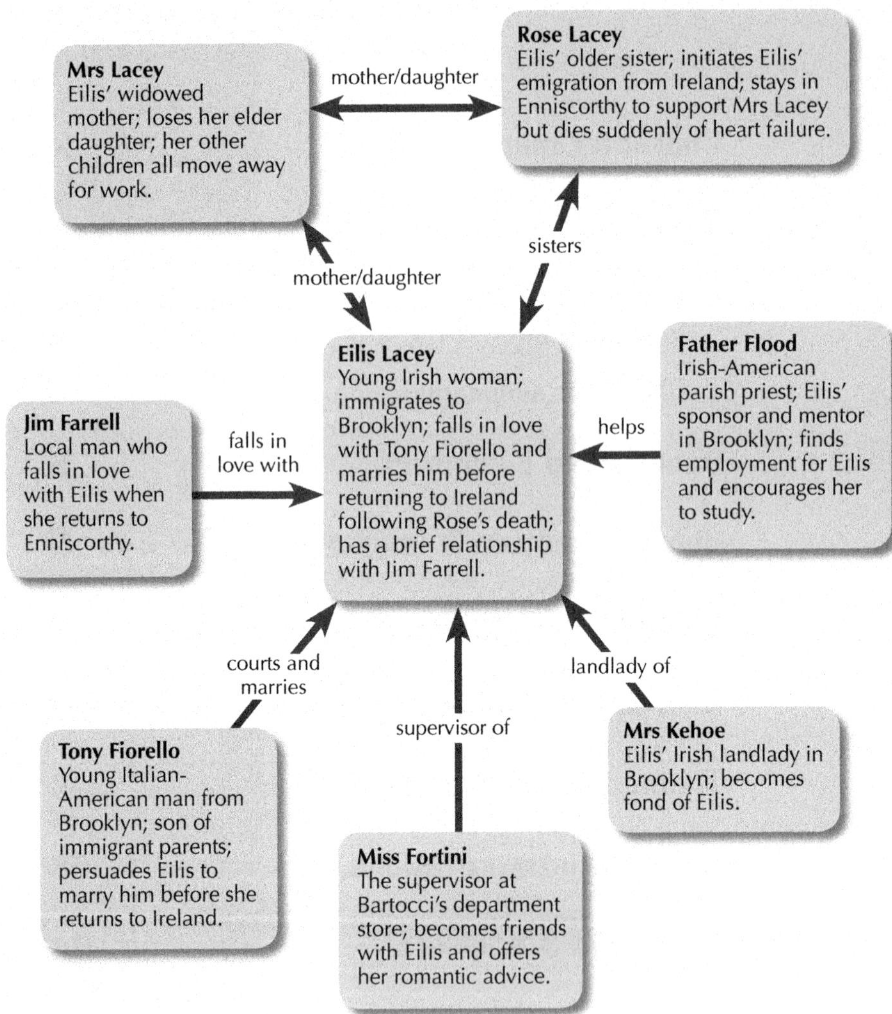

OVERVIEW

About the author

Colm Tóibín is one of Ireland's most admired contemporary writers. Born in Enniscorthy in 1955, he has travelled extensively and now resides in the United States. Tóibín is a member of Aosdána, an Irish association of artists, and has had close professional ties to a number of universities in England and America. He currently teaches at Columbia University, where he holds the Irene and Sidney B. Silverman Professor of the Humanities chair.

Tóibín has written seven novels and a range of other work, including two volumes of short stories, poetry, drama and a large body of nonfiction. He is particularly interested in exploring ideas such as contemporary Irish society, the migrant experience, identity, family relationships and creativity. *Brooklyn* was first published in 2009 to considerable critical acclaim, winning the Costa Novel Award and being longlisted for the Man Booker Prize in that year.

Synopsis

In the early 1950s, Eilis Lacey lives in Enniscorthy with her recently widowed mother and older sister, Rose. She is completing a course in bookkeeping, but there is no professional work available and the only employment she is offered involves serving part-time in Miss Kelly's shop. Rose introduces the family to an Irish priest, Father Flood, who lives in New York. He urges Eilis to consider immigrating to America. He offers to sponsor her and subsequently organises her accommodation and employment in Brooklyn. Despite Eilis' dismay at leaving home, she complies without protest when she realises that her mother and Rose are in favour of the scheme. Before crossing the Atlantic she meets up with her brother Jack, who lives in England. During the sea voyage to America, Eilis is violently seasick.

In Brooklyn, Eilis boards at Mrs Kehoe's and starts work at Bartocci's department store. She settles in well, but when she receives the first letters from Ireland she becomes very homesick. Father Flood suggests that she keep busy and enrols her at Brooklyn College to do a part-time bookkeeping and accountancy course. In turn, Eilis spends Christmas Day assisting with Father Flood's dinner for the homeless Irish.

In the new year, Father Flood starts running a regular parish dance to raise money for charity. Eilis attends, with the other boarders. She meets a young American-Italian man named Tony Fiorello, and they begin a relationship. Tony makes no secret of his feelings towards Eilis, but she is more circumspect. In the meantime, Bartocci's welcomes 'coloured' customers into the store for the first time, a controversial initiative that invites criticism from some of Eilis' fellow lodgers.

Eilis passes her first-year exams at Brooklyn College and commences the final year. She and Tony see each other frequently; she meets his parents and three brothers, and he takes her to Coney Island and to a baseball game at Ebbets Field.

Eilis receives the unexpected and shocking news that Rose has died in her sleep of a pre-existing but undisclosed heart condition. In her sorrow, Eilis turns to Tony. They sleep together for the first time and, before she returns to Ireland for a visit, secretly marry.

Back in Enniscorthy, Eilis tries to support her mother. Through her friend Nancy Byrne, Eilis reconnects with a local man, Jim Farrell. She tells no one of her marriage to Tony. What starts as a harmless flirtation with Jim quickly escalates into a potentially serious relationship. Confused and conflicted, Eilis realises that she has made a mistake in marrying so impulsively, but she still cannot bring herself to tell Jim the truth. When Miss Kelly, her previous employer, indicates that she knows of Eilis' deception, Eilis confesses her situation to her mother and returns to Brooklyn.

Character summaries

Eilis Lacey

The protagonist of *Brooklyn*; a young woman from Enniscorthy, Ireland, approximately twenty years old, who immigrates to America. In Brooklyn, Eilis works in Bartocci's department store and studies bookkeeping. During the course of the novel she is romantically involved with both Tony Fiorello and Jim Farrell.

Rose Lacey

Eilis' thirty-year-old unmarried sister; works in the office of Davis's Mills and supports Eilis and their mother financially. Rose encourages Eilis' emigration. She dies unexpectedly from an undisclosed heart condition.

Mrs Lacey

The mother of Rose, Pat, Martin, Jack and Eilis Lacey; widowed four years earlier.

Miss Kelly

The proprietor of a prosperous grocery shop; offers Eilis a part-time job.

Nancy Byrne

Eilis' closest girlfriend; she is about the same age as Eilis and works behind the counter in Buttle's Barley-Fed Bacon. She becomes engaged to George Sheridan.

Annette O'Brien

Another good friend of Eilis'; also of a similar age to Eilis.

George Sheridan

Nancy Byrne's fiancé; in his mid-twenties. Runs a successful shop in Market Square and will inherit the business in full after his mother's death. Member of the rugby club and close friends with Jim Farrell.

Jim Farrell

George Sheridan's closest friend; of a similar age to George and also a member of the rugby club. An only child who works in his father's hotel in

Rafter Street. Becomes romantically involved with Eilis when she returns to Enniscorthy.

Jack Lacey

Eilis' older brother; has followed his two brothers, Pat and Martin, to Birmingham for better employment prospects. Meets Eilis in Liverpool before she leaves for America.

Georgina

An Englishwoman with whom Eilis shares a cabin on the Atlantic crossing.

Father Flood

The Irish parish priest who facilitates Eilis' immigration to Brooklyn; acts as a sponsor and mentor when she arrives.

Mrs Kehoe

An Irishwoman from Wexford who runs a boarding house in Brooklyn. Deserted by her husband; takes Eilis under her wing.

Miss McAdam

An Irishwoman from Belfast; lodges at Mrs Kehoe's boarding house and works as a secretary.

Sheila Heffernan

Another Irish lodger from Skerries; Miss McAdam's friend. Works as a secretary.

Patty McGuire

A lodger at Mrs Kehoe's. Born in New York and works in a department store.

Diana Montini

A lodger at Mrs Kehoe's; Patty's best friend. Born in New York of an Irish mother and an Italian father.

Dolores Grace

An Irish girl from Cavan; works as a 'scrubber'.

Elisabetta Bartocci

Eilis' employer; daughter of Mr Bartocci, the owner of Bartocci & Company's department store.

Laura Fortini

The supervisor at Bartocci's and Eilis' immediate superior.

Joshua Rosenblum

Eilis' Jewish law instructor at Brooklyn College; a survivor of the Holocaust who lost his entire family during the war.

Tony Fiorello

The American-Italian man whom Eilis falls in love with and marries. Lives with his parents and three brothers in Brooklyn. In his early twenties; a plumber.

Laurence, Maurice and Frank Fiorello

Laurence and Maurice are Tony's older brothers. Frank is Tony's 'kid' brother; he is eight years old.

BACKGROUND & CONTEXT

Historical and social setting: Ireland

Eilis' departure from Ireland is part of an Irish exodus that saw emigration levels escalate dramatically after World War II. Ireland had become a republic in 1937, officially severing ties with Great Britain. Nevertheless, its policy of neutrality during the war had been unpopular internationally, and had the residual effect of marginalising the country economically and politically. Ireland did not share in the postwar boom enjoyed by most other Western economies; growth was sluggish and unemployment high. Consequently, over 400,000 people left Ireland in the 1950s to find work elsewhere. In *Brooklyn*, Eilis' three brothers immigrate to England, and Jack Lacey, when asked, dismisses the notion of permanently returning to his homeland because 'there's nothing there for me' (p.36). The other favoured destination for young Irish men and women wanting to find work was America.

Reference to the then Irish Prime Minister, Éamon de Valera, and his party, Fianna Fáil, indicates that *Brooklyn* is set in the early 1950s. These two names dominated Irish politics for most of the twentieth century. Fianna Fáil, the centre-right Republican Party, was founded in 1926 by de Valera, a leader in Ireland's struggle for independence. The party first came to power in 1932, and de Valera served multiple terms as head of government, working doggedly towards Irish home rule. After a short period out of office, Fianna Fáil regained power in 1951.

The Ireland in which Eilis has grown up is a deeply conservative society. It is essentially a theocracy in which the influence of the Catholic Church is profound. The law, as well as cultural and social attitudes, is informed by the Church's teachings. On issues such as marriage, divorce, contraception, sexuality and gender politics, there is no effective forum for debate or dissention. This has particular implications for women, who have no control over their fertility and are compelled to accept the dictates of the Vatican regarding birth control. Religious practices, such as regular attendance at mass and taking the sacraments, are scrupulously observed. The text raises the question: to what extent might the Irish Catholic Church's authority be diluted by the process of living in a more tolerant and secular community? While this is obviously dependent on the individual involved, *Brooklyn* does suggest that Eilis is freer to make her own decisions in America.

The influence of the Church, with its male hierarchy, reinforces the patriarchal nature of Irish society in the 1950s. The power structures – political, economic and domestic – are still, in the main, invested in men; in Eilis' world, decisions are made by priests and politicians. The majority of women do not go on to further study after school and few have aspirations beyond marriage. The fact that Eilis is seeking qualifications as an accountant, rather than working in a shop like her friend Nancy Byrne, earmarks her as clever and atypical. Married women become financially dependent on their husbands – indeed, many will be legally required to give up their jobs. The expectation is that they will stay at home with the children. After the Lacey brothers leave for Birmingham, Rose becomes the breadwinner and surrogate father – but, significantly, she seems to have relinquished all thoughts of marriage. Women of this generation are not encouraged to 'have it all'. It will be at least another decade before equal rights for women becomes a societal crusade.

Historical and social setting: Brooklyn

Brooklyn is the second-largest and most populous of New York City's five boroughs. Situated south of Manhattan, at the western end of Long Island, it is a city built on immigration – densely populated and ethnically diverse. Through the nineteenth and twentieth centuries, various groups emigrated from Europe, fleeing poverty and persecution. Russian Jews, Italians, Poles, Germans, Scandinavians and large numbers of the Irish all contributed to the multicultural flavour of the city. By the 1950s Brooklyn's Irish population was well established, as second and third generations had intermarried with other migrant groups. In the text, Diana Montini, with her Italian father and Irish mother, exemplifies the mix of ethnicities in Brooklyn.

One of the key elements that united this eclectic community was a baseball team, the Brooklyn Dodgers, whose games were held at Ebbets Field. The team inspired a fierce parochial loyalty, as Tony Fiorello and his brothers demonstrate. When the Dodgers relocated to Los Angeles in 1957, there was a palpable sense of loss among the Brooklyn community. Other iconic names associated with the area are referenced throughout *Brooklyn*. Coney Island, where Tony takes Eilis, is a beach and amusement park off the coast of southern Brooklyn that was extremely popular with New Yorkers up until the middle of the twentieth century.

In the 1950s, America was experiencing unprecedented economic prosperity. It was a decade of increased consumerism, advertising and selling; consequently, employment opportunities were extensive. The Irish network that already existed in Brooklyn – represented in the text by Father Flood – made it relatively easy for newcomers to adapt to their adopted country. Brooklyn itself was in a continual state of flux. The novel alludes to the shift in the borough's demographic as its industrial base of manufacturing and shipping started to wane. Miss Bartocci informs Eilis that 'New people arrive and they could be Jewish or Irish or Polish or even coloured' (p.59). At the same time, many families moved further out on to Long Island, and the ambitious plans expressed by the Fiorello brothers typify the urban development that was occurring at this time.

Eilis' world in Brooklyn is a relatively contained one. The narrative focuses on what is directly relevant to her and there is little mention of external affairs or the larger picture. Nevertheless, there is still some reference to the outside world that helps to contextualise Eilis' story. For example, *Singin' in the Rain*, the first film to which Tony takes her, opened in New York in March 1952. Similarly, although television had been in existence for a number of years, it did not become prevalent until the early 1950s. Mrs Kehoe's dubious concern over buying one – that 'it might not catch on and she'd be left with it' (p.176) – sounds comical with hindsight, but it reflects the scepticism many would have felt at the time.

One of the few times that Eilis' life intersects with an important social issue is with regard to the serving of black customers. In 1948 President Truman had affirmed the principle of equal opportunity and treatment for all armed servicemen, irrespective of race or colour. Mrs Kehoe reminds her lodgers that black soldiers had been killed in World War II 'just the same as our men ... No one minded them when they needed them' (p.117). However, it was not until 1954 that the Supreme Court ruled that racial segregation in public schools was unconstitutional, thus paving the way for widespread desegregation. And it was not until 1955 that Rosa Parks, a black woman, defied Southern practice and famously refused to give up her seat to a white passenger on an Alabama bus. This led to a decade of protest, but civil-rights violations were endemic, particularly in the South, up until the late 1960s. In *Brooklyn*, the idea of black customers mixing freely with whites – as well as being served by whites – is considered contentious enough to generate considerable debate outside Bartocci's store and 'fierce tension' within (p.112).

Enniscorthy

Enniscorthy – Colm Tóibín's birthplace and the setting for several of his novels – is an ancient town that dates back to the fifth century. It is the second-largest town in County Wexford, in Ireland's south-east, and has a population of approximately 9500. Enniscorthy has a number of well-preserved historical sites that signal its long history, including the imposing Enniscorthy Castle, built in 1205. There are several sporting amenities; a rugby club, to which Jim Farrell and George Sheridan belong; and an 18-hole golf course, where Rose would have played. Two local beaches, Curracloe and Cush Gap, are also featured in the text.

Hurling

The ancient Irish game of hurling is an extremely fast-paced combination of lacrosse, hockey, baseball and Gaelic football. Like these other team sports, it is played outdoors on a grass pitch. Hurling uses an axe-shaped stick called a hurley and a small ball called a sliotar, which can be struck, thrown or kicked. There are fifteen players to a team. Although the sport has now grown in international popularity, it was unheard of outside Ireland during the period in which *Brooklyn* is set. Tony's blank response when Eilis tries to draw a correlation between hurling and baseball reveals the American ignorance of the game in the 1950s. In fact, compared to the furious pace of hurling, baseball looks very sedate.

GENRE, STRUCTURE & LANGUAGE

Genre

Brooklyn is a deceptively simple rite-of-passage novel that explores the dilemma of being an expatriate – of losing one's home and then losing it a second time. The novel chronicles two journeys. The first is Eilis Lacey's literal voyage from Ireland to America. In the process, she undergoes a second journey, this one towards self-knowledge and maturity, moving from innocence to experience. Her world view broadens, she learns more about relationships and, most importantly, her understanding of herself expands.

The novel is also a romance. In Brooklyn, Eilis falls in love with Tony Fiorello and loses her virginity. However, when she returns to Enniscorthy, this relationship seems unsustainable and she becomes involved with another man, Jim Farrell. The fact that neither Tony nor Jim knows of the other's existence in no way detracts from the classic romantic triangle in which Eilis finds herself. She must choose between the two – and by extension, decide which kind of life she will have. Here Tóibín deliberately confounds readers' expectations. Having set up a classic conflict between love and duty, the ending of the novel takes an unpredictable turn. Rather than being obligated to return home and leave her new life with Tony, the fact that Eilis is married provides a twist and, therefore, she is compelled to return to America.

Structure

Eilis' crossing to America and back home again provides the structural framework of the novel. *Brooklyn*'s linear narrative is divided into four parts that cover the three clear phases of this journey. Eilis' time in America is book-ended by her departure from Ireland and her subsequent return. The timeframe covers approximately two years: Eilis arrives in New York in September 1951 and returns to Enniscorthy in June 1953. It is worth noting Rose Lacey's function as a narrative device. It is she who instigates Eilis' immigration to the United States, and it is her death that provides the incentive for Eilis' homecoming.

This carefully plotted, symmetrical structure reinforces the importance of place and of a sense of belonging. Whether she is in Ireland or Brooklyn, Eilis is subject to the restless disorientation that accompanies exile. For example, when she returns to Enniscorthy she feels as though the life she had established in Brooklyn 'had almost dissolved and was no longer richly present for her' (p.231). She struggles to recover 'what had seemed so filled with detail, so solid, just a few weeks before' (p.231). Consequently, her response to going back again is to become more and more fearful, and she seems to have come full circle: 'She would face into a life that seemed now an ordeal, with strange people, strange accents, strange streets' (p.232). This is not to trivialise her life in Brooklyn. Rather, it demonstrates the power of place and the intensity of Eilis' connection to home.

The novel is a study in contrasts, and the interplay, both literal and metaphorical, between Enniscorthy and Brooklyn underscores the duality of Eilis' experience. Tóibín emphasises this by juxtaposing a series of parallel images whereby Eilis finds herself in situations that deliberately mirror earlier circumstances. For instance, she goes to the beach and attends dances with both Tony and Jim. This juxtaposition invites readers to reflect on the differences – and similarities – between Ireland and America, as well as highlighting the choices that Eilis must make.

Language

Tóibín's precise, restrained prose eschews the use of metaphor. Those few metaphors that are deployed in the text are all the more memorable because of their infrequency. When Eilis suffers acutely from homesickness, anything seems preferable to facing her 'tomb of a bedroom' (p.70). The loss of her home represents a kind of bereavement, and the image conveys Eilis' sense of being overwhelmed by her feelings. The description of

Miss McAdam watching Eilis 'as though she were a prisoner on parole who might try to abscond' (p.101) succinctly suggests both Miss McAdam's suspicious personality and Eilis' defensiveness.

Generally, rather than using figurative language, Tóibín creates vivid images through his sustained use of detail. No one reading the description of Eilis' crossing to America, for example, could be in any doubt as to the disagreeable nature of travelling third class by boat:

> As she began to return to the cabin, longing to cover herself with blankets on the top bunk, hoping that no one would realise that she was the one who had made the mess in the corridor, the urge to be sick became even more intense than before, forcing her to get down on her hands and knees and vomit a thick liquid with a vile taste that made her shudder with revulsion when she lifted her head. (p.42)

Tóibín's style is almost journalistic. He reports Eilis' story with understated simplicity, and the steady accumulation of detail helps to bring the narrative to life. Despite the unassuming nature of the subject matter and the lack of obvious drama, momentum and emotional intensity are built as events unfold.

Tóibín's language choices are also, not surprisingly, informed by the fact that this is a novel about the Irish. Through dialogue, Tóibín knowingly captures the rhythms and phrasing of the Irish 'voice'. For example, Eilis and the other Irish characters rarely use contractions but tend to use more formal phrasing – Eilis asks Frank Fiorello, 'Would you not like that?' (p.150) – and certain idioms appear on a regular basis, irrespective of the speaker, such as 'that's all I have to say' (p.174).

The title

The title of the novel suggests that the text is as much about Brooklyn and its inhabitants in the early 1950s as it is about Eilis. If the novel explicitly explores Eilis' rites of passage, the setting of Brooklyn provides the catalyst and the forum. Tóibín references the dramatic shifts in Brooklyn's migrant demographic and, more specifically, hones in on the Irish experience as it relates to the city. Eilis changes profoundly when she moves there; the text's broader implication is that so do all newcomers to the area. Old lives are put on hold and different ones emerge. The challenge implicit in this experience is finding a balance between the past and the future, knowing what to surrender and what to retain. Eilis learns, in the course of her particular journey, just how difficult this is.

The Brooklyn the novel presents is confined to the relatively small portion that Eilis experiences. Like most newcomers to a city, her perceptions are limited. Busy with her job and her study, and knowing few people, Eilis does not really start to look beyond Mrs Kehoe's boarding house and Bartocci's store until she meets Tony. He introduces her to Coney Island and Ebbets Field, but the 'tourist' New York eludes her. Tóibín contends that this is typical of the migrant experience, where the newness of a place is intimidating and therefore the individual's 'emotional universe becomes the entire universe' (Knox 2010).

Nevertheless, Brooklyn is a microcosm of the wider world. Tóibín has said that part of the impulse for writing the novel was political (Morton 2009), and he presents a strong argument for the positive benefits of an open-door immigration policy. The underlying assumption is that multiculturalism adds value to a society. Brooklyn not only embodies a new beginning and additional opportunity for people such as Eilis, the Fiorellos and others, but their experiences also illustrate the societal advantages that emerge from diversity.

Tóibín conveys a strong sense of the city's vibrant, heterogeneous character. Eilis primarily mixes with other Irish, but she also studies with Jews, Russians, Norwegians and Italians at Brooklyn College, as well as interacting with an eclectic range of nationalities and ethnicities at Bartocci's. Through Eilis' marriage to Tony, her story becomes another archetypal Brooklyn story of conjoined cultures.

Narrative point of view

Brooklyn is written in the third person, but exclusively from the point of view of the protagonist. In the absence of an omniscient narrator, the intimate sharing of Eilis' experiences invites empathy from and collusion with the reader in much the same way as a first-person narration might. As the perspective is limited to this one character, the narrative viewpoint raises some of the same questions as a first-person narration with regard to reliability and accuracy.

Eilis is an intriguing heroine – self-effacing and guarded. She reveals herself through what she does and what she says to others – or sometimes does *not* say – rather than through any specific information she discloses about herself. We are not told of her likes or dislikes; we do not even know exactly how old she is or what she looks like. The gaps are filled in by what others, such as Father Flood and Tony, say about her. Throughout the novel Tóibín records Eilis' observations and reflections but, in the main, refrains from articulating her emotions, just as Eilis hesitates to express her feelings to others. Eilis is reluctant to give voice to what *she* wants from life. Rather, she allows others to make decisions for her. She is reactive rather than proactive; her point of view is diffident, and at times indecisive. This is very evident when she vacillates over telling the truth to Jim and her mother: 'She would try not to postpone any further what she had to do' (p.242).

The narrative perspective is generally reliable, reflecting Eilis' natural inclination to try to see any given mode of behaviour or set of circumstances fairly and objectively. When Mrs Kehoe offers her the new bedroom, Eilis overanalyses the agendas of those concerned, blaming everyone, including herself, until finally she comes to 'no conclusion except that it would be best if she stopped thinking about it altogether' (p.104). It is not in her nature to make value judgements, and she tends to resist casting blame. However, her understanding is limited by youth and inexperience, as well as by the variables of a strange new context. In this sense she is naive, and the narrative voice captures the limitations of her experience and understanding. For example, Eilis' lack of sophistication is demonstrated in the quasi-erotic episode with Miss Fortini. The latter's unforeseen behaviour elicits no comment from Eilis who, though surprised and embarrassed, is unable to decode the older woman's purpose with any certainty. It is left to the reader to draw their own conclusions.

CHAPTER-BY-CHAPTER ANALYSIS

Part One (pp.3–50)

Summary: *Eilis Lacey is offered a job serving in Miss Kelly's grocery shop; she accompanies her best friend, Nancy Byrne, to a dance; Rose Lacey introduces her mother and sister to an American-Irish priest, Father Flood, who facilitates Eilis' immigration to America; before leaving, Eilis meets her brother Jack in Liverpool; she has a difficult crossing.*

From the opening lines of *Brooklyn*, Eilis is established as an observer of life rather than an active participant – she watches her sister Rose through the window as the latter returns home from work, and she continues to look on 'silently' (p.3) as Rose gets ready to go out again. Whereas Rose is defined by her energy, there is a sense of stillness about her sister that suggests she is waiting for her life to truly begin. The image of Eilis as an onlooker is reinforced by the supportive role she plays as Nancy's companion, accompanying Nancy to the dance so that she can meet George Sheridan. Eilis has little interest in the weekly 'cattle mart' (p.17) herself.

Eilis has almost completed her bookkeeping classes, but the lack of employment opportunities in Enniscorthy places her in a kind of limbo. The work she is offered at Miss Kelly's, though menial, at least provides Eilis with a temporary financial incentive: 'It would be better than nothing and, at the moment, she had nothing' (p.6). It is clear, however, that neither Rose nor her mother approves of the job, which they consider beneath Eilis. Only belatedly, after Eilis has tried to make a joke out of working at the store, does she realise that her 'weekly humiliation' (p.24) is one of the key factors in her family's endorsement of Father Flood's proposition.

The role that Father Flood plays in facilitating Eilis' emigration highlights the extraordinary authority of the Catholic clergy in Ireland. Mrs Lacey is prepared to trust a relative stranger and delegate her youngest daughter's welfare to his care simply because of his position. During and after the discussion with Father Flood, Rose's uncharacteristic silence warns Eilis of the seriousness with which her family greets his proposal. The Laceys' emotional life is lived in the spaces created by these silences. This is a family whose intimate knowledge of each other still precludes frank and honest conversation: they 'could do everything except say out loud what it was they were thinking' (p.31). There is no consultation and no discussion of this decisive upheaval in Eilis' life – an improbable idea very quickly becomes a fait accompli.

Eilis' initial ambivalence at leaving her home soon becomes panic. She feels that she is being 'singled out for something for which she was not in any way prepared' (p.28). Yet, instead of resenting her mother and sister for their decision, Eilis' instinct is to protect them from her fears: 'There was, she thought, enough sadness in the house, maybe even more than she realized. She would try as best she could not to add to it' (p.31). Typically, Eilis avoids confrontation with those closest to her and represses her true feelings. Nor does she confide in Nancy or her other friends. Her peremptory dismissal by Miss Kelly suggests that she has already moved beyond the narrow confines of the life she has known so far.

Eilis is mindful that going to work in America is immeasurably different from simply moving to England. America is 'utterly foreign in its systems and its manners' (p.31), but it also has an 'element of romance' (p.32) that foreshadows unprecedented opportunity. Even the embossed notepaper on which Bartocci & Company offers Eilis a position seems 'heavier, more expensive, more promising than anything of its kind she had seen before' (p.26). The reality is that in Brooklyn, as in Enniscorthy, Eilis will still work in a store – albeit a much larger and more glamorous one than Kelly's. The offer from Bartocci's involves working on the shop floor, rather than a role that would deploy Eilis' fledgling bookkeeping skills. But its attraction is based on the potential for advancement and the security of permanent work.

America's allure, as well as the paradoxes that underlie its existence, is symbolised by the ocean liner that will carry Eilis across the Atlantic. It stands apart, 'massive and much grander and whiter and cleaner' (p.33) than the other ships around it. However, the contrast between the imposing facade and Eilis' cabin is marked. Deep beneath the waterline, in the belly of the ship, Eilis has to cope with cramped and airless conditions which are the antithesis of the gleaming exterior. Jack's comment that they 'eat their young in America' (p.34) highlights the alien, and potentially ruthless, nature of the land to which Eilis journeys. Her brother's admission that, at the beginning, he 'would have done anything to go home' (p.38) resonates with Eilis, foreshadowing the acute homesickness she will feel in Brooklyn.

Tóibín describes Eilis' dreadful crossing to New York in some detail. There is a grim irony in her assumption that the boat trip will be a holiday of sorts, sandwiched between the familiarity of home and the unwelcome business of arriving in a strange country: 'If only the rest of it could be as easy as this!' (p.38). The hierarchy on the boat reflects the societal divisions that also separate individuals in everyday life, and the tiny third-class cabin that Eilis shares with Georgina is a world away from the comforts of first class.

On the other hand, seasickness is a great democratic leveller, affecting the whole ship. Alone and ill, Eilis is thrown completely onto her own resources for the first time. She automatically thinks of the other people she knows – Georgina, Rose, her mother, even Miss Kelly – who might help. But she has 'no idea what to do' (p.41). A pattern is established as Eilis realises that she will never be able to tell anyone about the terrible night. Even though 'every moment of it was absolutely real, totally solid and part of her waking life' (p.44), she will not share the experience with her family. Eilis' true separation from the other Laceys commences at this point.

Key point

The fact that neither Jack nor Eilis can communicate their distress about emigrating to those back home illustrates the lonely nature of the migration experience. The real story of Eilis' rite of passage will, in the main, be denied to her family.

Key vocabulary

Mass: Roman Catholic church service. Weekly attendance at mass was considered compulsory for Catholics at this time.

Parish: the larger Catholic diocese, or district, of Brooklyn is divided into smaller ecclesiastical districts called parishes, each with its own church. Father Flood is a parish priest, and therefore has administrative and pastoral responsibility for the Catholics in his parish.

Q What are your first impressions of the Lacey family?

Q How does Tóibín establish a sense of time and place in this opening section?

Q What do we learn about overseas travel in the 1950s?

Part Two (pp.53–91)

Summary: *Eilis boards with Mrs Kehoe and starts work at Bartocci's; she experiences dreadful homesickness; Father Flood arranges for her to study bookkeeping and accountancy at Brooklyn College; Eilis works in the parish hall on Christmas Day, serving Christmas dinner to homeless Irishmen.*

Eilis' first three months in Brooklyn are anchored by two familiar elements: the Catholic Church, as represented by Father Flood's kindly presence; and the Irish ambience of Mrs Kehoe's boarding house. To some extent, these elements cushion Eilis and assist with her transition, but there is still much that is confronting about her new life.

Living in a community share house is an adjustment in itself. At Mrs Kehoe's, Eilis is 'the new girl, and the youngest' (p.57). While the majority of Eilis' fellow boarders are Irish-born, beyond this connection they are a disparate group, and Eilis keeps her emotional distance. The household gathers together for the evening meal, and this ritual of sitting at the dinner table is re-enacted throughout the text. It is an image that usually typifies family and intimacy, but in the circumstances depicted to this point in the narrative, communication is often forced. In Enniscorthy, Eilis had taken the opportunity to divert her mother and sister with mocking imitations of Miss Kelly. However, subsequent mealtimes had been full of 'too much talk and laughter' (p.28) as the family tried to evade the sad reality of another loss. At Mrs Kehoe's table, discussion is restricted to emerging fashion trends, and any reference to personal matters or politics is strongly discouraged. What characterises these dinner table conversations is, in fact, a lack of genuine connection.

Eilis' daily walk to Bartocci's from Mrs Kehoe's, through the quiet backstreets of Brooklyn to the bustle of 'the real world' (p.59), becomes increasingly strange, and parallels the journey she has made from Ireland. The actual work of serving in a busy department store is less of a challenge than the emotional fatigue of an overstimulated mind where 'each moment appeared to bring some new sight or sensation or piece of information' (p.58). Eilis intuitively seeks solitude whenever possible as a way of protecting herself against the heightened sensitivity that accompanies the day-to-day 'frenzy' (p.64).

If Miss Kelly's store is a typically Irish concern, servicing a small community and knowing its clientele intimately, Bartocci's is representative of the larger context of Brooklyn. These two businesses approach their respective clients very differently. Miss Kelly plays favourites and has 'a different tone' (p.9) for each customer, which oscillates between 'deep disapproval' (p.9) and a warm greeting. The best produce is reserved for her special patrons, and she is able to trade with impunity because of the essential lack of competition in Enniscorthy. On the other hand, it is impressed upon Eilis from the beginning that all of Bartocci's customers are treated exactly the same and must be welcomed 'like a new friend' (p.59). This practice is driven by shrewd pragmatism in a highly competitive marketplace. Bartocci's recognises the changing demographic of the borough and is not prepared to compromise its potential customer base: 'They all have money to spend' (p.59).

At the same time, Bartocci's also values its staff. Unlike Miss Kelly – who does nothing but criticise her hapless assistant Mary – Bartocci's management appreciates that 'the only way for the customers to be happy is for the staff to be happy' (p.60). There are generous financial incentives for employees to further their qualifications, and when Eilis' homesickness becomes apparent she receives nothing but kindness. The letters that Eilis receives from her family are relatively impersonal, but they trigger a series of vivid images of Enniscorthy that distress her deeply. Her dream about the Friary Hill courthouse carries confusing messages about the 'inconsolable' nature of her loss (p.67), as well as an underlying resentment that exacerbates her sense of estrangement: 'In her dream she found a way of avoiding her mother' (p.68). Bartocci's compassionate approach to Eilis' problem goes a long way towards helping her overcome it.

Father Flood's solicitous advice that she must keep busy opens another new door for Eilis. The cosmopolitan flavour of Brooklyn is reflected in the mix of students at Brooklyn College, where a number of different migrant groups are represented. Eilis' difficulty in distinguishing between the Jewish and Italian students reveals her unsophistication and parochial background. Yet unlike some of her peers, Eilis is willing to accept difference, and this exposure to diversity will become one of the richest legacies of living in New York. Eilis' status as one of the few women enrolled in the course is also a comment on the scarcity of professionally qualified women in the 1950s. Even in a large, progressive city such as New York, the majority of women do not have tertiary qualifications or work independently after marriage.

Key point

Eilis has the strength of character to put her homesickness behind her. Rather than allowing it to destabilise her life, she throws her energies into working hard, knowing that she is creating opportunities for herself.

Key vocabulary

Grace: the prayer said before a meal, thanking God for the food.

Ceili: traditional Gaelic folk music and dancing performed at social gatherings.

Q What are the immediate differences between Eilis' new life and her old one?

Q What examples of Eilis' growing self-sufficiency do we see in this part of the book?

Q Miss Murphy calls Father Flood's Christmas dinner 'the miracle of the turkey and the ham' (p.88). What is the 'miracle'? How important are social traditions in a new and different context?

Part Three (pp.95–199)

Summary (pp.95–139): *Mrs Kehoe offers Eilis a new room; Eilis and the other boarders go to Father Flood's parish dance; Bartocci's decides to welcome 'coloured' customers to the store; Eilis buys some new law books; she meets Tony Fiorello at the dance and quickly forms a relationship with him.*

Mrs Kehoe's reasons for offering Eilis the best room are ambiguous. On the one hand, she wants to reward Eilis: 'You are the only one of them with any manners' (p.99). At the same time, she wants to spite the other girls and forge an alliance with Eilis. Again, Eilis resists the intimacy proffered. Her response – she sees Mrs Kehoe's partisanship as 'a piece of gross presumption' and feels 'almost angry' at her approach (p.100) – is interesting in light of her loneliness. Mrs Kehoe's pointed slamming of the door at the end of their conversation is in marked contrast to her whispered preamble, showing that her displeasure has prevailed over discretion. The whole incident demonstrates that Eilis takes little at face value and dislikes the possibility of being in anyone's debt. In spite of her desire for 'a real friend' (p.103), she is intensely wary with regard to new relationships.

Father Flood's parish dance temporarily unites the boarders in a common interest. Even Miss McAdam and Sheila Heffernan, despite their usual reluctance to socialise, see it as a way of supporting a worthwhile charity. Father Flood's dance evokes the dances held back in Enniscorthy and is a celebration of Irish culture, with its Irish band and ceili music. The dance exemplifies the Catholic courtship ritual by which young members of the church meet and socialise in a controlled environment. In the 1950s, the protocol is firmly circumscribed by gender – the boys ask the girls to dance, never vise versa. Those who lack obvious appeal are consigned to the sidelines as 'wallflowers' (p.134) and have to wait out the dancing in silent humiliation. Eilis disparagingly equates it with a 'cattle mart' (p.105) and indeed, the young women have as little power as heifers being appraised for their market value.

It is indicative of Brooklyn's social elasticity that Eilis meets an Italian in this somewhat insular context. The dance is supposed to cater to members of Father Flood's parish, and the possibility of Italians attending is viewed with deep suspicion from conservative quarters. However, Eilis has no such reservations. Far from being deterred by Tony's background, she is intrigued, and willing to explore the relationship on its own merits. Both she and Tony are arguably stepping out of their respective comfort zones. Tony's casual reference to a family his parents know suggests that the Italian network is just as closely monitored as the Irish.

In the meantime, Eilis discovers that many assumptions held by the Irish with regard to America are unfounded. Winter in New York is unexpectedly bitter, and Eilis ruefully notes the irony that no one at home knew that America was 'the coldest place on earth and its people on a cold morning like this the most deeply miserable' (p.97). Another myth is shattered when Eilis visits Manhattan to shop for textbooks. Far from being as glamorous as most newcomers believe, Manhattan is just as 'dingy' and 'poor-looking' as Brooklyn (p.118).

It is under these circumstances that she is inadvertently confronted with a piece of her lecturer's tragic history. It is also one of the rare times that Eilis' lack of worldliness is explicitly set against the wider backstory of twentieth-century violence. Joshua Rosenblum – whom she knows only as an entertaining and erudite teacher – is the first Jew Eilis has met, and her ignorance regarding the Holocaust is obvious. It is understandable that Eilis has been sheltered from world politics, but the scene acts as a salient reminder that societies must remember and learn from their history, lest it be repeated.

Throughout *Brooklyn*, Tóibín explores the language of clothes and the way in which they can be a protective buffer against judgement or criticism. For example, Nancy Byrne, sensitive to the fact that many in

Enniscorthy might consider George Sheridan 'grander' than her (p.20), dresses with 'a great deal of trouble' (p.16) when she returns to meet him. Initially, Eilis is an unsophisticated young woman with little idea of how to dress. Yet she is keenly aware of what others wear and recognises the power of clothes to leave an impression. When the 'coloured' women enter Bartocci's store – from their perspective, uncertain and perhaps hostile territory – they have dressed with 'great care' (p.111). Eilis is struck by the effort they have taken to present themselves well: both are beautifully dressed in cream woollen coats and their hair is 'perfect' (p.112). Eilis' admiration for their clothes encompasses a recognition of the courage required for them to enter a white store. The idea that clothes can also represent specific qualities – either positive or negative – is reinforced when, later, Eilis effectively undercuts Sheila Heffernan's bigoted assumptions of superiority by drawing attention to her 'fussy old cardigans' (p.117) and unkempt appearance.

The change in Eilis' clothes symbolises her growing independence. In the past, Eilis has had Rose to guide her, and when Eilis disembarks at Ellis Island, she wears a dress that her sister has chosen for her. However, what seemed acceptable in Enniscorthy doesn't look appropriate in New York. Eilis concludes that the dress she wears to the first parish dance looks 'terrible' (p.106) and she 'would have given anything' (p.108) to be dressed as glamorously as Diana and Patty. Confidence comes with the right clothes, and Eilis is determined to buy something 'which would make her feel more like the girls she had seen dancing' (p.109).

Key point

Meeting Tony Fiorello will bind Eilis to America in a way that she could not have imagined before meeting him. She starts to see the city from a new perspective and to appreciate its possibilities.

Q Why is Eilis so resistant to Mrs Kehoe's friendship?

Q Comment on the significance of the Red Fox stockings being displayed separately to those bought by white women.

Summary (pp.140–99): *Eilis meets Tony's family; Miss Fortini helps Eilis to choose a swimsuit; Eilis receives notification that she has passed her first-year exams; Tony takes Eilis to Coney Island and a Dodgers' game; Rose dies unexpectedly in her sleep; before she returns to Ireland, Eilis secretly marries Tony.*

Eilis' emotional development is mirrored in the seasonal changes that chart the ebb and flow of life in Brooklyn. Throughout the harsh winter, she is cocooned by routine. By the time she has passed her first-year exams at Brooklyn College, Eilis is feeling more buoyant, and her mood is reflected in the flowering of spring. As the weather warms, her romance with Tony flourishes. However, she is troubled by the fact that he clearly means 'business' (p.137). She recognises that the relationship is moving too quickly for her, but is unsure how to slow it down without losing him altogether. In trying to analyse their situation objectively, Eilis concludes that 'she herself, in all her uncertainty and distance from him, was the shadow and nothing else' (p.144).

The motif of gathering around a table for dinner is revisited when Tony takes Eilis to meet his family – the first family meal that Eilis has shared since leaving Ireland. It is very different from dinners with her mother and sister, where thoughts are guarded and private grief is masked with gossip and storytelling. Eilis finds that in the Fiorello household there is very little privacy and everything is out in the open. She is warned in advance of younger brother Frank's 'real big mouth' (p.146). Eilis is welcomed like a daughter, but she feels uncomfortable at being 'on display' (p.150) and being 'presented to them as something more than a girlfriend' (p.146). Nevertheless, despite her ambivalence, she is inevitably drawn into the Fiorello orbit.

Tony taking Eilis to Coney Island is a milestone in their relationship. The location is a socially acceptable place in which young people can explore their sexuality under the guise of swimming and sunbaking. Tony affirms his ownership of Eilis before they set off: 'I'll have to tie a rope around you' (p.158). Despite Eilis' extensive preparations – or perhaps because of them – she is nervous and self-conscious about stripping down to her swimsuit in front of Tony. By contrast, she is in her element in the water.

Coney Island beach faces the Atlantic Ocean and, as such, has sizeable waves and a strong current. Tóibín uses the sea as a metaphor, representing the choices available to Eilis. The American waters seem very mild compared to the cold Irish Sea, but Eilis, a competent swimmer, realises the dangers in their unfamiliar depths and understands that she will need to be careful. The waves are 'stronger' (p.160) than at home and threaten to pull her out to sea, potentially casting her adrift. By extrapolation, her new life presents hitherto unknown challenges that have the capacity to cause harm. Nonetheless, Eilis has options that Tony does not, as he cannot swim and fears the water. The desire to keep Eilis close – he 'hated her swimming away from him' (p.160) – reflects his underlying insecurity and foreshadows their impulsive marriage.

Eilis' first baseball game at Ebbets Field is another initiation into the life of the city. Whereas she had previously been oblivious to the 'frenzy' (p.162) that grips Brooklyn during the baseball season, she now discovers how important it is to those who live there. For the Fiorello brothers, the Dodgers' success is a life-and-death issue and, during the game, Tony's preoccupation is such that he can 'no longer manage the role of caring, thoughtful boyfriend' (p.164). Eilis' position as an observer again comes into play. She watches the game and Tony's passionate absorption in it with an almost clinical detachment: 'The idea that he would never see her as she felt that she saw him now came to her as an infinite relief, a satisfactory solution to things' (p.165). For Eilis, there is a kind of reassurance in the knowledge that the relationship does not require her to let down her emotional guard and is unlikely to penetrate her emotional defences.

Rose's untimely death is both a crisis and a turning point for Eilis: 'It changed everything Eilis thought about her time in Brooklyn; it made everything that had happened to her seem small' (p.177). Eilis' shock and distress are compounded by her physical distance from her remaining family. Her immediate response is to voice regret at coming to Brooklyn, but she cannot undo what Father Flood tells her any more than she can 'push back time' (p.171). Eilis feels as if 'all of the colour had been washed out of her world' (p.178) and it is no accident that she turns to Tony for comfort. However, in offering him sexual proof of her commitment, she makes it more difficult for either of them to walk away from the relationship. Eilis, typically, tries to accommodate the emotional pressure that comes from two mutually exclusive interests – her grieving family and her apprehensive boyfriend. Inevitably, in acquiescing to Tony's proposal of marriage, she compromises herself.

Tony's offer is made for all the wrong reasons – he argues that 'if we don't do it, I'm going to go crazy' (p.196) – and his logic that marriage carries the same weight as a simple promise is disingenuous. Yet Eilis' assurance that she will return to Brooklyn also highlights the way in which complex emotional variables can easily be underestimated. While Eilis means what she says, she does not have the experience to imagine how quickly circumstances might change.

Key point

In the short term Rose's death brings Eilis and Tony closer together, but Eilis' decision to return to Ireland separates them in a way they have not previously experienced.

Key vocabulary

Confession: the Catholic sacrament that will absolve Eilis of the mortal (serious) sin that, in her view, both she and Tony have committed.

Irish Wake: the traditional social ceremony that takes place in the house of a deceased person. Mourners view the body and celebrate the life that has passed.

Rosary: another ceremony associated with a Catholic death. The rosary is an evening of prayer that is usually said the night before the funeral.

Q Discuss Eilis' relationship with Miss Fortini. What does the bathing-suit scene reveal about each of these women?

Part Four (pp.203–51)

Summary: *Eilis supports her mother; she discovers that Nancy is engaged to George Sheridan and will shortly marry; Eilis starts spending time with Jim Farrell, who makes no secret of his attraction to her; she is offered work at Davis's Mills; Eilis regrets her hasty marriage to Tony, but ultimately decides to return to Brooklyn.*

Eilis is unprepared for the initial lack of empathy she feels for her old home. She had presumed it would be 'easy' (p.204) to return to Ireland. However, rather than experiencing relief and happiness, she feels disorientated and guilty, and 'all she could do was count the days before she went back' (p.205). It is her first insight into the divided emotional legacy that will accompany exile. Furthermore, without Rose as the buffer between them, Eilis is made aware of Mrs Lacey's selfishness. She shows no interest in Eilis' life in America, and is increasingly querulous and demanding of Eilis' time. Her blatant assumption that Eilis will remain in Enniscorthy for Nancy's wedding is driven by her own desires, rather than by any consideration of her daughter's arrangements or obligations.

In Enniscorthy, Eilis' appearance and, in particular, her American clothes excite comment. Given that Eilis' new wardrobe reflects her increased self-possession, it is significant that she now rejects Rose's clothes 'finally and emphatically' (p.213), telling her insistent mother that she does not want any of them, 'no matter how elegant they were or how much they cost' (p.213). The red-and-white costume that Eilis wears to Nancy's wedding owes more to Miss Bartocci's influence than her sister's. The disconnect between Eilis' life in Brooklyn and her life in Enniscorthy becomes more pronounced with her decision not to confide in her mother, or even her close friends, about her marriage. This diminishes America to 'a sort of fantasy, something she could not match with the time she was spending at home' (p.217).

On the face of it, everything seems to fall into place. Eilis is offered the kind of job she could only dream about while working on the shop floor in Bartocci's. Her silence also has the unforseen consequence of encouraging Nancy to matchmake on Jim Farrell's behalf. As a result, she is courted by a man who offers her emotional and financial security, as well as the opportunity to remain in Ireland. Through Jim, Eilis is afforded social access to a part of Enniscorthy that was previously denied to her – such as the restaurant of the Courtown Hotel – and the experience is exciting.

Tóibín again contrasts Eilis' experiences in Brooklyn and Ireland, highlighting the alternatives that face her by placing her in a parallel situation. Her visit to the beach with Jim mirrors the similar outing with Tony, and the subtext clues us in to Eilis' choices in a similar way. Unlike the visit to Coney Island, where her insecurities were on display, at the beach at Curracloe Eilis feels 'oddly confident' (p.215), comfortable in her own skin. On the second beach visit, to Cush Gap, she is even more relaxed. The Irish Sea is not as testing as the Atlantic, and Eilis enjoys its waters; she had forgotten its 'purity and calmness' (p.225). Unlike Tony, Jim is a strong swimmer, but he does not assert ownership over Eilis as Tony did. Instead, he is careful not to force any physical intimacy and 'almost as an aspect of this care, he made his interest in her totally clear' (p.225). Later, when Eilis looks back on the photograph that encapsulates this day, the image seems to validate their credentials as a couple by accentuating their reciprocal, untroubled enjoyment of each other's company.

The motif of the dance – symbolising hope and the promise of romance – is another deliberately juxtaposed image. Whether it is the boisterous ceili 'free-for-all' (p.129) performed at Father Flood's dance or the more sedate pace set on the Courtown dance floor, the common element is the dancers themselves and the music that brings them together in mutual expectation. When Eilis and Jim dance together, the fledgling relationship moves to a new level of intimacy. Eilis decides that he is 'handsome, graceful, smart, and, as the night wore on, she was proud to be with him' (p.228).

Tóibín charts Eilis' painful trajectory towards self-knowledge with sympathetic precision. Spending time with Jim Farrell makes her realise that she is no longer in love with Tony and that she has made a grave mistake in marrying him. Nevertheless, the question of what is real and what is not remains an unresolved issue for Eilis. Her relationship with Tony is reduced to a shadowy delusion:

> He seemed part of a dream from which she had woken with considerable force some time before, and in this waking time his presence, once so solid, lacked any substance or form ... (p.237)

Paradoxically though, Eilis understands that once she is back in Brooklyn, it is Enniscorthy that will seem 'like a strange, hazy dream to her' (p.251). Eilis' dilemma demonstrates the seductive lure of place and the primal urge to put down roots. Whichever choice she makes will involve sacrifice and loss. The decision to return to America, made under duress and with great regret, suggests that Eilis will permanently relinquish her Irish homeland. Whether she must also forfeit her autonomy and long-term happiness is a lingering question mark.

Key point

Ironically, Enniscorthy now seems to offer the promise and opportunity that was initially expected of America, but neither Eilis' conscience nor her sense of responsibility will allow her to stay in Ireland. The choice to return to Brooklyn demonstrates the extent to which she has grown in independence and maturity.

Q Is the time spent with Jim essentially a holiday romance?

Q Does Eilis' decision to return to Brooklyn show strength or weakness?

CHARACTERS & RELATIONSHIPS

Eilis Lacey

Key quotes

'I hear you have no job at all but a great head for figures.' (Miss Kelly, p.5)

'They said you were doing great here and Mrs Kehoe says you're the nicest girl she's ever had staying ...' (Father Flood, p.74)

'Irish girls aren't like Italian girls. They're serious.' (Tony, p.133)

Initially, Eilis' role is a passive one. As the youngest in the family, she has been used to her parents and older siblings making key decisions. There is an implicit recognition that she is a talented young woman – Eilis 'never made mistakes when she did addition' (p.61) – and should have the chance to further her skills. Even so, immigrating to America is entirely Rose's initiative and, as Rose and Mrs Lacey collude with Father Flood, Eilis feels 'like a child' (p.23) whose fate is being decided for her. Somehow it is 'tacitly arranged' (p.23) that she will leave Ireland. Eilis loves her family too much to challenge the proposal, however resistant she might privately feel; nor is it in her nature to do so. Tóibín has this to say of his heroine:

> Eilis is someone who by her nature is a second daughter. She's not brave, and has always had everything important done for her. Everything about her is withheld. She is holding her breath, as if she's afraid that by breathing out she'll offend someone. (Tóibín 2010)

Accordingly, Eilis is so ill prepared for the experience of leaving home that she cannot even identify the subsequent melancholy that overwhelms her. Homesickness is a 'terrible weight' (p.66) that underscores her anonymity in Brooklyn: 'She was nobody here ... she was a ghost in this room, in the streets on the way to work, on the shop floor' (p.67). At the same time, Eilis quickly realises that she must adjust if she is to survive. This means embracing the various elements of her new life and suppressing her longing for Ireland: 'It would be like covering a table with a tablecloth, or closing curtains on a window' (p.76).

Eilis' independence and resilience are revealed gradually. Thrown onto her own resources, she has to exercise her judgement and make critical choices with little guidance or support. Her initial naivety is balanced by natural curiosity and a determination to learn. She takes the opportunities provided to educate herself and, as the world opens up before her, embraces new ideas with less diffidence than before. Living in New York encourages assertiveness, and Eilis becomes more inclined to trust herself. At work, she learns to be 'brave and decisive' (p.113).

The fact that Eilis is chosen by Bartocci's to serve black customers is a significant compliment, although she may not see it at the time. In being asked to serve these women, Eilis has again been 'singled out' (p.112) for something for which she feels ill prepared. However, the administration has recognised her capacity to accept difference and adapt to changes that others find confronting. She also brings to the divisive scenario something of the neutrality of the outsider. Her fair-minded response highlights a strong sense of social justice, and when she rebuts the officious Sheila Heffernan, she is able to do so with humour as well as assurance, deliberately distancing herself from the prejudices of the other woman.

Eilis is, by nature, reserved and emotionally guarded. She is selective in her relationships and shies away from physical intimacy. It is not easy for her to express her true feelings, even to those closest to her. This is particularly evident in her relationship with Tony where, initially, she is held back by apprehension and doubt: 'His saying that he loved her and his expecting a reply frightened her' (p.143). Despite her genuine enjoyment of Tony's attentive and sympathetic company, Eilis recoils from the implication that she might be a permanent exile and that 'this was the only life she was going to have' (p.143). Eilis needs to be able to set her own pace and work through issues in her own way. The day after Rose's death, she is determined to return to Bartocci's in spite of her sorrow. She manages to continue her routine, including the evening classes: 'She was careful on the shop floor and proud that not once did she break down or have to go suddenly to the bathroom and cry' (pp.178–9). Her characteristic response is to grieve in private.

Returning to Enniscorthy, Eilis slips back into the rhythm of the town easily and finds comfort in its familiar faces and rituals. Yet the changes produced by her experiences in America are obvious to all. 'Everything about you is different', her friend Nancy insists: 'You seem more grown up and serious. And in your American clothes you look different. You have an air about you' (p.230). Eilis' poise and self-assurance intimidate her mother, whose strategy is to pointedly ignore any reference to her daughter's new life. Jim Farrell, on the other hand, is smitten.

When Eilis does not have the confidence – or the hard-headedness – to act on her instincts, she makes mistakes. The foremost is her impulsive marriage to Tony, but her treatment of Jim Farrell is another. Throughout the text, her actions are generally informed by the twin values of connection to family and a clearly defined sense of duty. Her generosity is a constant, and Tony rightly calls her 'a good person' (p.196). Yet the internal conflict generated by her return home causes her to lie by omission and to behave with great cruelty towards the unsuspecting Jim. Her bitter knowledge that first love is transient highlights the shadow that has always lurked on the edge of her relationship with Tony. By contrast, her feelings for Jim, born out of common values and a shared culture, appear to carry greater promise. However, while Eilis flirts with the idea of divorce, she never seriously considers the possibility of staying in Ireland. In accepting that she has done something 'foolish and hurtful' (p.237), she retains her essential integrity and the reader's sympathy.

Key point

Immigrating to America provides Eilis with the opportunity to grow and learn. But it creates an ongoing tension as to where her home is and where she really belongs.

Tony Fiorello

Key quotes

'He did not seem Irish to her; he was too clean-cut and friendly and open in his gaze.' (p.128)

'... this was a different world and in this world Tony shone despite the fact that his family lived in two rooms or that he worked with his hands.' (p.168)

'He is a good man.' (Eilis, p.190)

Tony is an engaging young man who radiates warmth and good humour. He is a plumber by trade, although Eilis learns that in Brooklyn 'it was not always as easy to guess someone's character by their job as it was in Enniscorthy' (p.140). She is conscious of the fact that Rose would make pejorative (negative) assumptions as to 'what a plumber looked like and how he spoke' (p.139), but Tony does not conform to this stereotype. On the contrary, Eilis is proud of his 'casual good manners' (p.139) and the social ease he demonstrates in company. Miss Fortini is so impressed by Tony's qualities that she advises Eilis to hold onto him: 'There aren't two of him. Maybe in Ireland, but not here' (p.141).

Despite the clear bond between Tony and his family, he stands apart from his brothers by virtue of his physical appearance. Whereas they all 'look like Italians' (p.146), Tony has blond hair and 'clear blue eyes' (p.126) that look out on the world with curiosity and amusement. Eilis is immediately drawn to him, though she is not sure at first whether she should distrust his transparent charm: 'He was not like anyone else she had ever met' (p.139). His candour and emotional directness are new to her, and very different from her own reserved approach to life. Tony engages completely with the given moment – whether that moment involves a funny film, a story of personal misfortune, or a loss by his beloved Dodgers. Eilis also recognises his emotional vulnerability early in their relationship.

Tony makes it clear from the start that he is serious with regard to Eilis. He is ready to settle down and, with his brothers, has ambitious plans for the future. Although he is tactful, and considerate enough not to rush Eilis sexually, he wants more emotionally than she is ready to give. She is frightened by his intensity and realises that he is 'moving faster' than her (p.143) and towards a different outcome than she envisages. Despite his love for her, Tony behaves selfishly towards Eilis when he coerces her into marriage. His fear of losing her overrides good sense and, uncharacteristically, he does not look Eilis in the eye when he presents the proposal. Ultimately, neither of their interests is served by the premature commitment.

Father Flood

Key quotes

'He's nice to those he's nice to.' (Mrs Kehoe, p.78)

'Most people who come to this house without notice need something or have a problem ... You hardly ever get pure good news.' (Father Flood, p.156)

Father Flood plays a pivotal role in Eilis' new life. By extension, he represents the influence exercised by the Catholic Church on devout Catholics such as the Laceys. It is Father Flood who sponsors Eilis' immigration to America, and he subsequently acts as her mentor in Brooklyn. He takes a personal interest in her welfare and recognises her debilitating homesickness when it arises. He also appreciates her aptitude, facilitating her entry into Brooklyn College: 'I told them how brilliant you were' (p.77). There is a pragmatic aspect to Father Flood's goodwill: helping Eilis promotes the Church's mission in the United States. His comment that 'we need Irish girls in Brooklyn' (p.78) reveals this secondary agenda.

Shrewd and avuncular (like an uncle), Father Flood's sphere of influence is wider than might be expected. He has built up a useful network of friends and contacts and, by his own admission, 'can pull strings most places' (p.75). The fact that he has managed to get Eilis a highly coveted full work permit, rather than the usual temporary visa, suggests that he has some important connections. A believer in deploying 'the power of the collar' (p.75), Father Flood's modus operandi is to extract from the rich to give to the poor. Accordingly, he persuades a wealthy parishioner to pay Eilis' tuition fees: 'He needed to do something for mankind' (p.156).

Father Flood has a subversive streak and readily admits 'I love breaking all the rules' (p.75). His genial manner irritates Mrs Kehoe, who compares him to the Italian priests and wishes he was 'more dignified' (p.78). Her acerbic comment that 'it's about time someone spoke up to him' (p.78) alludes to his unclerical tendency to do things his own way. Nevertheless, Father Flood achieves a great deal of good in the community, particularly in supporting Irish expatriates in Brooklyn. Like all good residents of the city, he is a passionate supporter of the Brooklyn Dodgers.

Mrs Lacey

Key quotes

'She had used a tone that she had heard her mother use, which was very dry and formal.' (p.78)

'She's never slept a night on her own in the house and she keeps saying that she won't be able to.' (Jack, p.180)

Mrs Lacey is a quietly determined woman with a strong sense of propriety. The lessons on courtesy that she has imparted to her two daughters become part of Rose and Eilis' own mode of discourse. Mrs Lacey's life is lived through her girls, particularly Rose. She carefully tidies and cleans Rose's room every morning, cooks 'special' teas that accommodate Rose's busy social life (p.3), and takes an admiring interest in her wardrobe. Mrs Lacey supports Eilis' emigration because she believes that it is in her daughter's interests – and, of course, Rose's company seems assured. Like Eilis, Mrs Lacey is reticent with regard to sharing her emotions – characteristically, she bottles up her grief at losing Eilis to America. It is only when Eilis overhears a conversation with a neighbour that the depth of her mother's feeling is revealed.

The Lacey children are inclined to protect their mother from any information they feel may upset or worry her. For example, Rose suggests that Eilis write to her separately about 'private matters' (p.66). Consequently, Mrs Lacey is ill equipped to manage independently, and her helplessness is exposed after Rose's death: 'I have no one at all now, Eily, I have no one' (p.174). Grief and loneliness exacerbate her self-absorption. When Eilis returns home, Mrs Lacey's strategy is clear, and she can barely conceal her delight at her daughter's budding relationship with Jim Farrell. Her instinct is to avoid direct confrontation, but she is subtly manipulative in the way she encourages Eilis to stay in Enniscorthy. However, the sanctity of marriage is an immutable fact for Mrs Lacey, and once she knows of Eilis' situation she accepts the reality that she will lose her daughter again with careful dignity.

Rose Lacey

Key quotes

'Eilis was proud of her sister, of how much care she took with her appearance and how much care she put into whom she mixed with in the town and the golf club.' (p.11)

'Rose was the essence of efficiency and is much missed.' (Mr Brown, p.229)

In the absence of males, Rose has become the head of the Lacey family, as it is her income from Davis's Mills that supports her mother and sister. Consequently, both defer to her. Rose has carved out an alternative, and apparently contented, life for herself. Most of her peers are married with children, but Rose, while she enjoys an active social life, has resisted settling down. At thirty, she grows 'more glamorous every year' (p.11), and she sustains this stylish image through judicious shopping at Dublin's biannual sales. Like her mother, Rose has a strong sense of how to behave and is mindful of her family's position in the town. Her presence and gracious manners usually ensure the best of treatment, as Eilis discovers on their last day together, in Dublin. Even Rose's handwriting, with 'its clarity and evenness, its sense of supreme self-possession and self-confidence' (p.177), conveys her strength and poise.

It is only in hindsight that Eilis realises Rose's diplomacy and the extent to which she 'handled' their mother, encouraging her interest in 'even the smallest detail' (p.209) of her daughters' lives. Rose is equally loving towards Eilis, and supportive of her career goals. She pays for the books that Eilis requires for her course and has tried to find her younger sister suitable work at Davis's. Although her own lifestyle is settled and conservative, Rose is prepared to encourage her sister to be daring, and she is the driver behind Eilis' emigration. Eilis wishes that Rose, 'so ready for life, always making new friends' (p.30), would exchange places with her. However, perhaps influenced by her health concerns, Rose is prepared to sacrifice her own prospects. In typical Lacey fashion, she chooses not to confide in the other family members about her heart condition and doggedly continues her normal regime: 'Maybe she was very brave', her mother tells Eilis (p.173).

Eilis looks up to her glamorous and confident sister with an admiration that borders on worship. Indeed, Rose's spirit pervades the narrative to a greater degree than her actual presence might suggest, if for no other reason than she exercises a profound influence on her younger sister. Eilis has been content to play second fiddle to Rose all her life – she tells Tony that Rose was considered 'the most beautiful' in their family (p.178). Eilis has modelled herself on her sister and regularly strives to emulate her tone of voice and mode of behaviour, stating 'Rose was a great example to me' (p.229).

Mrs Kehoe

Key quotes

'Changing fashions and new trends were her daily topic ...' (p.54)

'When you've gone through the world like I have ... you'll find that that [honesty] only works some of the time.' (Mrs Kehoe, p.100)

Mrs Kehoe is Eilis' landlady in Brooklyn. She has been deserted by her husband and left with little means of support. Consequently, she has had to compromise her previously affluent lifestyle to survive. Her 'deep resentment against the world' (p.100) is generally kept carefully in check, concealed beneath an impeccably groomed exterior. Her regular poker game is the social highlight of her week, but it is portrayed to Eilis as 'another form of Sunday duty that she performed only because it was in the rules' (p.54). Mrs Kehoe runs her Irish boarding house with an iron fist, even directing her lodgers' conversation over the evening meal. Though she takes a keen interest in clothes and shoes, she draws the line at 'any mention of boyfriends' (p.54) or politics, for which she has a 'complete revulsion' (p.56).

A woman of decided opinions, Mrs Kehoe takes an immediate liking to Eilis, approving of her good manners and restraint. However, Mrs Kehoe's favour is a mixed blessing. When she allocates 'the biggest, the warmest, the quietest and the best appointed' room in the house to Eilis (p.96), her preferential treatment threatens to alienate the other girls. It also unsettles Eilis, who is suspicious of her landlady's motives and anticipates that there may be a price to pay. As Tony comments to Eilis, 'that woman looked like she owned you' (p.133).

Deeply conservative and a staunch Catholic, Mrs Kehoe lives according to strict moral principles. Her outrage when Eilis commits the cardinal sin of letting her boyfriend stay the night threatens to completely destabilise their relationship. Eilis' contravention is 'in the realm of the unthinkable' (p.188). Nonetheless, despite Mrs Kehoe's autocratic facade, she is in many respects a lonely individual with a soft heart, and her genuine regard for Eilis eventually overcomes her disapproval.

Jim Farrell

Key quotes

'He's only bad-mannered when he's nervous ... He doesn't mean it. He's a big softie.' (Nancy, p.222)

'And there would be neighbours, Eilis thought, who already were aware that she had been seeing Jim Farrell and would view him in the same way as her mother did, as a great catch ...' (p.234)

An only child, Jim is the son of a wealthy publican. He is a reserved, cautious young man whose shyness is often mistaken for arrogance. Certainly, his initial dealings with Eilis leave her with a very poor impression of him, and his offhand rudeness to her reinforces the perceived social distance between them: Rose says, 'He sounds like a pup all right' (p.20). The transformation in his manner when Eilis returns to Enniscorthy disconcerts her, and his deliberate courting highlights the extent to which she has absorbed some of America's 'glamour' (p.227). Eilis' early misgivings dissolve and, despite her reservations, she soon finds herself enjoying his company.

The image Jim presents is sophisticated and assured. When Eilis compares him to Tony, he seems 'less eager ... less funny, less curious, but more self-contained and more sure of his own place in the world' (p.236). She appreciates his tact and impeccable manners. However, Jim is more emotionally vulnerable than he appears and has always found it difficult to make friends. Nor has he had great success with women. Jim likes Eilis sufficiently to admit his inadequacies to her and makes clear his desire to continue the relationship, suggesting 'maybe we could get engaged before you go' (p.241). Later though, after Eilis has encouraged his attention, she realises that his position in the town and his essential conservatism preclude any future together: 'He had never done anything unusual in his life, and, she thought, he never would' (p.242).

Laura Fortini

Key quotes

'Miss Fortini was interested only in timekeeping and tidiness and making sure that the slightest complaint or query was immediately conveyed to her.' (p.62)

'Miss Fortini was always watching ...' (p.169)

Eilis' initial contact with the enigmatic Miss Fortini is when the latter writes, on the store's behalf, with the job offer that will take Eilis to Brooklyn. Her handwriting, which is 'clear and beautiful' (p.26), conveys something of Bartocci's authority. As the store's sharp-eyed supervisor, Miss Fortini watches everyone and misses nothing. She is efficient and exacting – in the frenzy of the nylon sale she appears to be able to oversee the entire proceedings, despite being 'not especially tall' (p.64). Miss Fortini is the first person to notice Eilis' homesickness, and acts on it with kindness and pragmatism.

Miss Fortini has a less than satisfactory Italian boyfriend and advises Eilis, who considers her 'intelligent and interesting' (p.141), on the expectations of Italian men. Nevertheless, their growing friendliness in no way prepares Eilis for the unexpected interest Miss Fortini takes in her choice of swimsuit. Does Eilis recognise the sexual connotation implicit in the older woman's behaviour? In spite of Eilis' inexperience, she is made to feel extremely uncomfortable and knows that there is something unnerving about Miss Fortini's scrutiny that she will 'never be able to tell anyone about' (p.154). Given Miss Fortini's position as Eilis' immediate superior, her advance signals an opportunistic abuse of power that is, somewhat cynically, predicated on the younger girl's naivety and compliance.

THEMES, IDEAS & VALUES

The migrant experience

Key quotes

'She had a sense ... that, while the boys and girls from the town who had gone to England did ordinary work for ordinary money, people who went to America could become rich.' (p.24)

'... it was like the arrival of night if you knew that you would never see anything in daylight again.' (p.70)

America is perceived as the land of opportunity and promise – it offers the lure of a prosperity that is unobtainable in Ireland or England. But there is also a price to pay: despite its 'compensating glamour' (p.32), it is not as accessible as England; people do not come and go, returning home as the whim takes them. Having left the country of their birth, new arrivals are swallowed up by America's magnetism and energy: people were 'happy there and proud' (p.24). By implication, there is no turning back.

Like the other Irish, Eilis believes that 'while people from the town who lived in England missed Enniscorthy, no one who went to America missed home' (p.24). Her brother Jack hints at the difficulties of immigration, but nothing prepares Eilis for the disorientation she experiences once in Brooklyn. It is not until her second year that she begins to feel some empathy for her new home. Walking the streets, she observes 'how beautiful' the city is and realises that she has 'never felt like this before in Brooklyn' (p.155). Yet hers will be the migrant inheritance – she will always feel like 'two people' (p.218), divided by conflicting attachments and loyalties.

Father Flood has reassured Eilis' mother that parts of Brooklyn are 'just like Ireland' (p.23). The Irish in exile cherish their national heritage – they celebrate traditions, re-enact familiar rituals and reminisce among themselves. Mrs Kehoe loves nothing better than to talk about the hurling matches back in Wexford or Sunday trips to the beach at Curracloe. Even the food she serves at her boarding house is 'too Irish', according to Diana Montini. The Church is the glue that cements this community together, and much of Irish expatriate life centres on the parish, 'even more than in Ireland' (p.23).

In this context, Father Flood has a significant role to play – the parish dance, with Pat Sullivan's Harp and Shamrock Orchestra, is one of his initiatives. Its dual purpose is to raise funds for charity and to provide an opportunity for young Catholics to socialise. The Christmas dinner Father Flood organises for the 'leftover Irishmen' (p.84) is another example of the Church's pastoral care. The situation these men are in highlights the displacement that can accompany migration. Most have severed all contact with Ireland, but, after decades in America, they have nothing to show for their time away. Christmas Day is their one opportunity to reconnect with their language and memories.

The delicate balance between valuing one's traditional heritage and assimilating successfully is not always easy to maintain. Many migrants will live in a cultural ghetto and cling to the reassuring safety of the familiar. Miss McAdam and Sheila Heffernan, for example, give every impression of wearing permanent blinkers – they are unwilling to tolerate anything they find different or challenging. The homogeneity of many migrant cultures, including that of the Irish, ill prepares them for the eclecticism of New York. Miss McAdam expresses the narrow-mindedness of those who are affronted by Brooklyn's diversity: 'I didn't come all the way to America, thank you, to hear people talking Italian on the street or see them wearing funny hats' (p.56). However, she brandishes her own Irish-Catholic conservatism like a cudgel.

By inviting us to interrogate such comments, Tóibín presents tolerance as a crucial value, without which a society loses direction. Tolerance is one of the strengths that underpin a robust and vibrant democracy. Joshua Rosenblum's case demonstrates America's traditional role in providing a haven for those who need to escape persecution. His story also exemplifies the way in which talented individuals are absorbed into the fabric of a tolerant society to mutual advantage.

Furthermore, *Brooklyn* highlights the importance of adaptability, resilience and emotional strength. These are qualities that every migrant needs – without them, survival is difficult and success is impossible. The aspirational Fiorello family, with their optimism and willingness to work hard towards long-term goals, exemplify the American dream in action. They have arrived from the Old World, decimated by war, with nothing but their energy and clannish loyalty. Tony's parents and brothers share a modest two-roomed apartment, but their ambitions are large. The three eldest sons have had the initiative to buy land on Long Island, which the brothers will develop by working collaboratively. The youngest, Frank – 'the brains of the family' (p.149) – will go to college. Each member of the family has an important role in contributing towards their upward mobility. In time, Eilis will become a part of this transformation.

Key point

For those who leave their homes to start a new life in a foreign place, the two critical constants are faith and family. Often these values assume even greater importance than before and help to establish a sense of belonging in a new community.

Social divisions

Key quotes

'Some of the shopkeepers in this town ... I don't know why they think so highly of themselves.' (Mrs Lacey, p.20)

'I heard there are coloured women going into Bartocci's ...' (Miss McAdam, p.116)

Social hierarchies operate in both Ireland and America. In Enniscorthy, ownership is considered the principal determinant of worth and there is a clear understanding of the layers that make up the town, from those who 'sweep the streets' (p.10) to the shopkeepers who 'think so highly of themselves' (p.20). The locals keenly monitor these social divisions. Hence Nancy Byrne experiences undisguised snobbery when she starts going out with George Sheridan – he is part of the rugby set and his 'sort' (p.7) usually stick to themselves.

Eilis notices the transition in her friend's demeanour as her marriage approaches, and she realises that Nancy has deliberately primed herself for her new role as Mrs George Sheridan – a role 'that would count for something in the town' (p.227). At the wedding, the contrast between Mrs Byrne's 'unseemly' inebriation (p.238) and Mrs Sheridan's 'immense dignity' (p.237) underlines the difference in status between the two families. Eilis' mother is critical of the townspeople's pretensions, yet she cannot hide her deep satisfaction at the possibility of her daughter being romanced by Jim Farrell. His initial rudeness to Eilis is forgiven as Mrs Lacey imagines a connection with one of Enniscorthy's most prominent families.

Despite the generosity extended to migrants, Eilis discovers that parts of American society are deeply divided. In particular, the division between black and white is stark and entrenched. The lodgers at Mrs Kehoe's make their racism clear as the social barometer starts to shift. Interestingly, it is a migrant business, Bartocci's, which challenges the code of social apartheid and makes the contextually radical decision to welcome black customers. Eilis is told that 'there is a change going on outside the store' (p.110) and that it will be mirrored within Bartocci's. New blood can provide new perspectives and a new way of doing things. Bartocci's, with its open-door policy, symbolises America's expansive immigration program. Owned by Italians, staffed by Irish, and welcoming 'every single person who comes into this store' (p.59), it is a metaphor for the fusion of cultures that pass through Ellis Island.

However, America welcomes the bigoted as well as the open-minded. The migrants who come to Brooklyn frequently bring their prejudices with them, and these ferment in the cultural melting pot. Miss McAdam and Diana Montini form an unlikely alliance in their mutual disapproval of Dolores Grace, the 'scrubber from Cavan' (p.122). Even Eilis is reluctant to be seen at the dance with her when Dolores appears dressed as 'a horse-dealer's wife in Enniscorthy on a fair day' (p.123).

Moreover, as a community of migrants, Brooklyn is obviously susceptible to social division, and the city is not without its tensions. Frank Fiorello's assertion that 'We don't like Irish people' (p.148) references the simmering hostility that exists between some migrant groups. This is exacerbated by the heavy-handedness that can be exercised by the predominantly Irish police force. Father Flood intimates that different groups appear to have different priorities; for example, the Jews value education, while the Italians are 'busy making money' (p.77). This might suggest that the various ethnicities in Brooklyn function as a series of parallel loops that only occasionally intersect. On the other hand, Eilis' own experience – ranging from studying at Brooklyn College to her interaction with the Fiorello family – sees her learn much about the heterogeneous nature of the area.

Change

Key quotes

'It struck her as she crossed the street that by the time she arrived home at six thirty a whole world of things would have happened ...' (p.58)

'... there was no guarantee that they would go on making programmes and she did not think she would take the risk.' (p.176)

Change, whether it is dramatic or incremental, is clearly confronting for those involved. *Brooklyn* argues strongly that if change is to be beneficial, it must be accompanied by a positive mindset. However, change is often forced on people through adverse circumstances, and they are not necessarily able to respond with equanimity. After Mr Lacey's death, his wife and children must make significant adjustments. For Eilis and her brothers, opportunity offsets the displacement of migration. By contrast, Rose's death leaves Mrs Lacey unable to rationalise the losses she has sustained. For her, change brings nothing but sorrow.

Throughout the novel, Tóibín both explicitly and implicitly compares the two very different cultures of Brooklyn and Enniscorthy; the first is defined by change, the second is seemingly impervious to it. Eilis has grown up in a small homogeneous community that shares a common ethnicity and religion. In New York, she is confronted with so much that is foreign that for each day, she 'needed a whole other day to contemplate what had happened' (p.58). Compared to the sleepy pace of Enniscorthy, everything seems 'frenzied and fast' (p.58). At Bartocci's, which acts as a kind of social barometer, the volatility of the context is acknowledged. Eilis is told that 'Brooklyn changes every day' (p.59); by extension, those who service this community must also be flexible and accommodating.

The 'makeover' that Eilis receives from Georgina shortly before they both disembark at Ellis Island foreshadows the ways in which she will be changed by America, both physically and emotionally. At the time Eilis feels ambivalent, disguised by Georgina's handiwork, and she has a prescient sense that she could lose her former self if she is not careful. On the other hand, there is also the suggestion that she might reinvent herself – the possibility of presenting a new and different face to the world. The tension between these two options is played out in Eilis' subsequent story. Moreover, the two men with whom she becomes romantically involved represent the alternatives offered to her regarding change and continuity.

Tony is a young man on the move. He is making his own way in the world, and his life will be very different from that of his parents. Like Eilis, Tony is naturally curious and receptive to new opportunities. He meets Eilis by attending the dance targeted at Father Flood's Irish parishioners. Inevitably, the relationship with Tony broadens Eilis' understanding of another culture. As Tony's girlfriend, she is introduced to new foods, new ways of thinking and even a different brand of Catholicism. Tony's disclosure that not all Italian priests who hear confession understand English startles Eilis. From her perspective, this trivialises the sacrament, but it underscores a more relaxed approach to 'sin' than that promulgated by the Irish clergy. When Eilis does make her confession to a young Italian priest, she finds him unexpectedly empathetic.

Making the choice to sleep with Tony signifies Eilis' emerging independence. It flies in the face of the teachings that have shaped her upbringing but, although she wants the Church's absolution afterwards, she is comfortable with her decision. At the time, she feels that intercourse with Tony makes a difference to her 'beyond anything she had ever imagined' (p.187). Yet when Eilis returns to Ireland, she reverts to the cautious, compliant girl of the past. Her new brave and confident self is repressed, and instead she feels like 'Rose's ghost' (p.218). Once again, she takes the line of least resistance: rather than breaking through her mother's self-absorbed shell and being honest about the relationship with Tony, Eilis allows things to drift. She promises herself that she will discourage Jim, but it is easier to pretend: 'She looked at his kind face ... and decided that she would tell him nothing now' (p.242).

Unlike Tony, Jim is set to inherit the life of his parents. As their only child, he has been groomed to take over Farrell's Hotel and is disinclined to oppose that legacy. Eilis recognises that he is deeply conventional: 'He liked his position in the town, and it mattered to him that he ran a respectable pub and came from a respectable family' (p.242). Arguably, Eilis' capacity for growth would be inhibited in Ireland. Settling down in Enniscorthy may bring financial security, but would require her to comply with conservative familial and societal expectations. The overarching context is narrow, with the Catholic Church defining the boundaries of behaviour and imposing rigorous constraints on independent discourse.

If America has opened up opportunities for Eilis, Ireland threatens to close them again. Notwithstanding the sweeteners implicit in the concept of home, it is possible that Eilis has moved beyond the narrow parameters offered by her previous life. Despite Jim's sincerity, the future he is offering Eilis is a predictable one that accords with much earlier aspirations: 'She had expected that she would find a job in the town, and then marry someone and give up the job and have children' (pp.27–8). Conversely, by the time she returns to Enniscorthy, Eilis' perspective has changed dramatically and she wistfully contemplates the possibility of working long-term. It is her experience in America that has encouraged this shift.

Love

Key quotes

'... he was special ... she was not staying with him simply because he was the first man she had met.' (p.168)

'It occurred to her ... that she was sure that she did not love Tony now.' (p.237)

Eilis' loneliness and inexperience makes her susceptible to falling in love. She sorely misses the comfortable intimacy of long-standing friendships, and Tony steps into this role before becoming her lover. Without realising the extent of her emotional vulnerability, Eilis allows herself to be carried along by his infectious enthusiasm for life and genuine appreciation of her. However, Tóibín foreshadows the true nature of the relationship when Eilis rationalises that she is not staying with Tony simply because he is the first man she has met. It is revealing that she does not mention him in letters home to her mother. The fact is, Tony *is* the first man she has gone out with and, in her naivety, Eilis mistakes her liking for love. She shrinks from marriage in the immediate future, but does not have the resolve to deflect Tony's proposal. Her affection for him overrides her judgement and she allows herself to be persuaded by his anxiety into making a commitment before she is ready.

Eilis' essential 'niceness' is her Achilles heel, and *Brooklyn* provides a poignant lesson in the importance of resisting emotional pressure. Once she has married Tony, given the social context of the 1950s and Eilis' own conservative Catholic background, she would essentially be trapped. Divorce seems inconceivable – the exclusive prerogative of film stars such as Elizabeth Taylor. Eilis concludes that the only answer to her predicament is that there is no answer, and 'nothing she could do would be right' (p.236).

Eilis' flirtation with Jim is out of character. She is neither unkind nor careless by nature, but her actions towards him are partly driven by his obvious admiration for her. It is worth noting that she hasn't been able to set her own pace in these two relationships at any point. Like Tony, Jim is on the rebound and is driven by a combination of impulsiveness and insecurity. Like Tony, he rushes Eilis into making a commitment – one that is tacit rather than explicit, but still meaningful.

Eilis perceives Tony and Jim 'as figures whom she could only damage, as innocent people surrounded by light and clarity, and circling around them was herself, dark, uncertain' (p.237). As she has done in the past, Eilis sees herself as the shadow, and it is typical that she blames herself for being flattered by the attentions of the same man who had previously rejected her. The text delineates the mercurial nature of young love. Eilis finds the speed with which the details of her life in Brooklyn recede alarming, and she no longer thinks of her husband as a 'loving and comforting presence' (p.232). Instead, everything about Tony seems 'remote' (p.231). Nevertheless, the attraction that she feels towards Jim may prove to be just as short-lived.

Does Eilis make the right choice? Both Tony and Jim can offer her something worthwhile. As Eilis is leaving Enniscorthy, she muses that, in time, her return to America 'would come to mean less and less' to Jim and 'more and more to herself' (p.252). While this certainly suggests that she will reflect on her decision with regret, even longing, it also implies something about America itself: it offers prospects that Ireland does not, and by making a new life there, Eilis will make the more dramatic change to her destiny. Eilis' resolution of her dilemma is not conclusive, and Tóibín intends this ambiguity. Ostensibly Eilis returns to Tony, but the removal of her wedding ring may suggest a more independent future – an option only permissible in the more liberal context of American society.

Key point

The disconcerting sense of unreality that Eilis feels towards Ireland and Brooklyn respectively, depending on where she finds herself at the time, feeds into her two romantic relationships. Just as the place that Eilis leaves becomes an unreality when she is elsewhere, so too does the relationship associated with that place fade into apparent insignificance, compared to the one in the immediate moment.

Loss

Key quotes

'She kept thinking ... that was like how she felt when her father died and she watched them closing the coffin, the feeling that he would never see the world again and she would never be able to talk to him again.' (p.67)

'She had lost all of them.' (p.70)

Brooklyn explores the melancholy legacy of loss and the many ways in which it can destabilise individuals. Collectively, the Lacey family experiences a cruel combination of death and displacement. Although Eilis' father has died four years earlier, the impact of Mr Lacey's death on his youngest child is such that she even imagines seeing him again in Brooklyn. Rose's shocking and unexpected death is a further trauma for the whole family – particularly for Mrs Lacey, following so closely the loss of her husband. To a devout Catholic such as Eilis' mother, death brings everlasting life; she is sustained by the belief that her loved ones are 'up in heaven praying for all of us' (p.209). From a practical perspective, however, Mrs Lacey is left completely alone.

Through Eilis, the text examines the critical loss of place and what it means to lose one's home and country. Before leaving Enniscorthy, Eilis recognises the enormity of the upheaval and senses that her future life will be 'a struggle with the unfamiliar' (p.30). She would have given anything to switch places with Rose, but is unable to express her dismay to her older sister. Rose, in turn, effectively surrenders the opportunity to have an independent life. In many ways she seems the more suited to emigrate, but instead is prepared to take on the future care of their increasingly dependent mother. Indeed, the recognition of Rose's altruism makes it harder for Eilis to refuse the opportunity presented to her.

Eilis' very real fear that she will lose everything she knows and loves is accompanied by a more subtle kind of loss – the loss of personal identity, of being recognised for who she truly is. Eilis has lived in Enniscorthy all her life. It is a small, tight-knit community where individuals and families know each other, if not directly, then at least by reputation. Father Flood's attempt to make a personal connection with Mrs Lacey on their first meeting is indicative of the close tentacles that anchor Irish relationships. By contrast, in exile in New York, Eilis is miserably conscious of her disconnection: 'Nothing here was part of her' (p.67). She feels forsaken by her family: 'Maybe ... they had never known her, any of them, because if they had, then they would have had to realise what this would be like for her' (p.71). It seems impossible to disclose her loneliness to them.

Accordingly, like Jack before her, Eilis deliberately censors her letters home, editing out any material that may cause her mother or sister to worry. Eilis' return to Ireland does nothing to alleviate this sense of alienation. She feels as though she has two separate identities: one who has lived in Brooklyn for nearly two years, and the Irish Eilis whom everyone knows – 'or thought they knew' (p.218). Even her own mother seems a stranger.

Eilis' story is being played out all over Ireland. The Laceys are victims of the postwar Irish diaspora, and the bleak employment landscape means that many families must reconcile themselves to the loss of their children in a similar way. Family units become fragmented and dislocated. In the weeks before Jack Lacey leaves for Birmingham, his mother and sisters 'would do anything to distract themselves from the thought that they were losing him' (p.28). The same sense of bereavement accompanies Eilis' departure.

In *Brooklyn*, loss is interwoven with sacrifice. The renunciation of personal desire leads only to emotional pain for the individuals concerned, as the immediate outcome is the tangible loss of a much-loved presence. Mrs Lacey's hopes that Eilis will return to Ireland permanently are shattered when she discovers her daughter's secret marriage. This time, driven by her Catholic values as well as by convention, Mrs Lacey has no choice but to sacrifice her own happiness and let Eilis go.

The trials of the Lacey family are set against an even broader social context. The postwar evacuation from Europe has seen hundreds of thousands of displaced people relocate with little but their memories. Many have come to America and, in particular, to Brooklyn. The loss that comes from social upheaval is therefore a persistent element in the lives of many of Eilis' contemporaries. Her law lecturer, Joshua Rosenblum, lost his entire family during the Holocaust. A shocked Eilis is told that the Germans 'murdered every one of them' (pp.119–20) and learns that Rosenblum's background exemplifies the tragic paradigm experienced by a generation of European Jews.

Key point

The text continually highlights the difficulty of really knowing other people, and of sharing one's true self and being understood. The change in Eilis, as she is shaped by a new life forged outside the local frame of reference, means that she has moved permanently beyond the emotional reach of friends and family.

Family

Key quotes

'Rose sent me a list of instructions, and they included one that said no kissing and hugging.' (p.33)

'... it would mean that they could soon, all of them, have a much better life.' (p.167)

Tóibín explores the two contrasting sides of Eilis' experience through a series of parallels. Thus, the loss of Eilis' Irish family is in part compensated for by her symbolic adoption by the Fiorello family. While the text demonstrates the ongoing value of familial support, the clear differences between the Laceys and the Fiorellos suggest that family, as well as providing an emotional anchor, can also impact on individuals in negative ways.

The fracturing of intimacy within the Lacey family has more to do with their tendency to suppress their emotional responses than their geographical dislocation. Eilis' caution with regard to relationships may be traced back to her family's inability to communicate their emotional needs. Although they are caring towards each other, the Laceys are not a demonstrative family. For example, when Eilis meets Jack in Liverpool, she is unsure whether to embrace him: 'They had never embraced before' (p.33). Tóibín deliberately omits Eilis' first leave-taking from her mother, and this exclusion contributes to the sense of emotional distance between them. The letters that Eilis receives from home tell her 'little' – there is 'hardly anything personal in them and nothing that sounded like anyone's own voice' (p.66). Whether from sorrow or resentment, Mrs Lacey spends Eilis' last forlorn night in Enniscorthy behind closed doors and refuses to see her daughter off the next morning. This is despite not knowing when, or even if, she will see Eilis again.

By comparison, the Fiorellos are warm, emotionally generous and inclusive. They share themselves as readily as they share their table. Their emotional closeness is symbolised by their physical environment – the tiny, cramped apartment in which they literally live on top of each other. As far as Frank, the youngest, is concerned, this arrangement is perfectly satisfactory; Eilis notes, with some surprise, his ambivalence at the possibility of *not* sharing a bedroom with his older brothers.

The Fiorellos' relocation to America has done nothing to threaten the strength of the family dynamic. The brothers' future plans involve pooling their professional skills, and Eilis' marriage to Tony will involve living on Long Island in close proximity to his parents. This is not necessarily very different from a marriage to Jim Farrell, which would have seen Eilis live only a few streets away from her own mother. Nevertheless, in marrying Tony, Eilis will also marry into a strong, co-dependent family network. For someone with Eilis' circumspect personality, raised in a very different sort of family, the Fiorellos' open-hearted lack of reserve is challenging: 'She loved them, each of them ... but sometimes she found the pleasure of being alone after a lunch or a supper with them greater than the pleasure of the meal itself' (p.166).

Key point

Tóibín is interested in the ambivalence that underpins many relationships. Through a protagonist who is often uncertain what she thinks about people or how to respond, he explores and acknowledges the shades of grey in relationships, and especially in family relationships.

The meal that Eilis shares with the Fiorellos before returning to Ireland reinforces her singular standing within the family. At this 'special lunch' (p.198), there is a decided sense of occasion. The Fiorellos have done Eilis the compliment of dressing more formally, and they make it clear that her 'safe return' (p.198) is a sincere priority. The lunch also demonstrates the extent to which Eilis has been influenced by exposure to Tony's family. Compared to the first, rather awkward, introduction, Eilis now feels so comfortable within the family circle that she almost hopes that Tony had confided in his parents about their clandestine wedding. The 'good cheer' (p.198) of this lunch and the effort made is a marked contrast to the meals Eilis subsequently has with her own mother. Mrs Lacey's deliberate avoidance of any meaningful conversation is such that Eilis begins to dread 'the silences between them' (p.217). She sees her mother with new eyes and wonders resentfully if she had 'always had this way of speaking that seemed to welcome no reply' (p.205).

While nothing can replace the family that Eilis has essentially lost, the acceptance she receives from the Fiorellos does help to offset the emotional deficit. The absence of her three brothers is partially assuaged by Laurence, Maurice and Frank. With the latter, she will experience the novelty of a younger sibling. Tony's mother – the only woman in this family of men – is a shadowy but sympathetic figure. Younger than Eilis' mother but older than Rose, Mrs Fiorello fuses the roles of surrogate mother and elder sister. It is she who initially warns Tony to take the relationship seriously, and she who, the first time they meet, asks Eilis about her studies and future plans. Her influence on her sons is so strong that at the Dodgers' game they obey to the letter her instructions not to marginalise Eilis. After

Rose's death, Mrs Fiorello attends Rose's commemorative mass with Tony and worries about Eilis. Tony's comment, 'Nothing is any trouble now' (p.177), illustrates the unqualified level of support that Eilis can expect from the Fiorello family and the regard with which she is held by them.

DIFFERENT INTERPRETATIONS

Different interpretations arise from different responses to a text. Over time, a text will give rise to a wide range of responses from its readers, who may come from various social or cultural groups and live in very different places and historical periods. Responses by critics and reviewers can be published in newspapers, journals and books, both online and in print. They can also be expressed in discussions among readers in the media, classrooms, book groups and so on.

While there is no single correct reading or interpretation of a text, it is important to understand that an interpretation is more than a personal opinion – it is the justification of a point of view on a text. To present an interpretation of a text based on your point of view, you must use a logical argument and support it with relevant evidence from the text.

Critical viewpoints

Colm Tóibín is a highly regarded novelist, an 'expert, patient fisherman of submerged emotions' (Schillinger 2009), and *Brooklyn*'s critical reception was very favourable. Reviewers have been unanimous in their praise for the novel's graceful, controlled prose, and Eilis' story has been seen as a sensitive and realistic depiction of the migrant experience.

Tóibín's evocation of place is considered one of the novel's greatest strengths. Liam McIlvanney, writing for the *London Review of Books*, contends that 'the ability to vivify imagined worlds is central to *Brooklyn*'s success' (McIlvanney 2009). While it is to be expected that Tóibín would depict his hometown with authority, the fact that he is equally familiar with New York City during the early 1950s is more of a surprise: for Jonathan Yardley in *The Washington Post*, 'the period feeling of *Brooklyn* is genuine and impressive' (Yardley 2009). Yardley also praises the thematic resonance of the novel and suggests that, despite its apparent modesty of scope, as a study of the search for home, *Brooklyn* has 'a universality that goes far beyond the specific details of Eilis' struggle'.

Reviewers have largely been united in their sympathy for the unassuming protagonist. Christopher Tayler, in *The Guardian*, maintains that Tóibín 'writes well about women, often putting them centre stage, and about people who feel compelled to hold their feelings at a distance' (Tayler 2009). Tayler also notes, interestingly, that Eilis is 'less defenceless and more troubled than she initially seems', which challenges the generally held view. Tóibín himself calls her a 'character in a "minor key"', one of those heroines who are 'well-mannered, shy, hard-working, careful of what they say' (Knox 2010). Nevertheless, Eilis' passivity has been criticised by some readers. Indeed, one admits that 'there were many moments when I wanted to wring her neck' (Baines 2010).

Finally, Robert Hanks, writing for *The Telegraph*, expresses some reservations about the ending, arguing that the emotional dilemma faced by Eilis is not 'properly fleshed out' (Hanks 2009). Hanks' response highlights the different ways in which readers can respond to elements of any given text.

Two interpretations of *Brooklyn*

Interpretation 1: *Brooklyn* shows the close connection between Irish life and Catholicism.

Brooklyn demonstrates the way in which ingrained cultural values are transposed from country to country. For the Irish, Catholic faith is fundamental to their cultural heritage. They have come from a society that has promoted a strong, pervasive and consistent morality. Catholicism has shaped their thinking and helped to define their national identity. For first-generation Irish immigrants, confronted with the strangeness of an alien culture, it is particularly important to retain this inheritance.

Irish Catholicism is transplanted to the United States with all of its vigour and commitment intact. Catholics attend mass regularly and take the sacraments, such as communion and confession, at their local parish church. At Mrs Kehoe's boarding house, grace is a habitual feature of every meal and the girls' morals are scrutinised from an Irish Catholic perspective. Father Flood's role as parish priest carries immense authority – even the Jewish principal at Brooklyn College stands 'to attention ... like it was the army' (p.77). Father Flood's parishioners come to him for advice and support, practical as well as spiritual, and his influence is considerable. His benign intervention in Eilis' life extends to scrutinising her boyfriend, at Rose's behest. Marrying outside the Church – a 'mixed' marriage – was anathema to the Catholic hierarchy of the 1950s, as was divorce. Father Flood's parish dance is therefore designed to offer young people a social outlet that will encourage lasting partnerships within the Irish-Catholic orbit.

The trajectory of Eilis' life is partially defined by the powerful values of patriarchy and religious belief. The idea of migrating to America becomes viable simply because it has been recommended by a priest, and when Father Flood speaks, Eilis' mother listens with 'cowed respect' (p.23). Eilis' values have been inculcated by her Catholic upbringing; the charity that she demonstrates in giving up her Christmas Day to assist the homeless is one example. Less positively, other actions arise from a substantial dose of Catholic guilt. Her decision to return to Ireland after Rose's death is triggered by Jack's letter and the knowledge that her mother is alone: 'I think she wants you to come home' (p.180), he tells her.

In fact, many of Eilis' choices are essentially made for her by the Catholic Church. She returns to her husband in Brooklyn because the idea of divorce is unconscionable: denunciation would follow, not from the secular American society in which she lives, but from her Irish-Catholic circle. It is not possible for Eilis to turn her back on the principles instilled by a Catholic conscience.

When tragedy strikes, Irish Catholics turn to their faith, wherever they are. In Ireland, the protocol that accompanies a death is defined and stage-managed by the Church. Rose's grieving family say the rosary for repose of her soul, they attend her wake and bury her with a requiem mass. Mrs Lacey even whispers an act of contrition into her dead daughter's ear in the hope that her sins may be forgiven.

Similarly, the Church in Brooklyn assumes ownership over Rose's death. News of the tragedy is carried by the clerical grapevine – Father Quaid in Ireland contacts Father Flood, who automatically steps into the role of carer. After breaking the news to Eilis, he arranges to telephone her mother at the Manse in Enniscorthy. It is a given that the rituals being played out in Ireland will be duplicated in Brooklyn. Accordingly, Father Flood holds a special mass for Rose, attended by Mrs Kehoe, Tony and his mother, and Eilis herself.

Brooklyn emphasises the close connection that the Irish have with their faith, whether in Ireland or New York, and illustrates the powerful and enduring influence of the Catholic Church on its followers. If anything, exile strengthens a cultural and religious bond forged from infancy. The Church provides both spiritual continuity and a valuable support network that helps to assuage the migrants' sense of displacement.

Interpretation 2: *Brooklyn* demonstrates the way in which Irish Catholicism can be affected by migration.

Irish Catholics who relocate to other parts of the world encounter societies that are very different from their own. *Brooklyn* shows how the diversity that migrants experience can dilute the narrow focus of Irish Catholicism. Contact with alternative belief systems broadens perspective and invites many to question, even challenge, religious assumptions that have previously been taken for granted.

Brooklyn, as Eilis discovers, is not the monoculture that Ireland is, and the Catholic Church no longer has a monopoly on people's hearts and minds. Different ethnicities have brought with them different religions and cultural viewpoints – Jews and Muslims, Buddhist and Orthodox all rub shoulders with Christians. Christianity itself is multidimensional, and many denominations co-exist alongside each other. Even the quintessential Christian festival of Christmas is expendable to some; Mrs Kehoe observes that in parts of Jewish Brooklyn 'it could be any day of the week' (p.82). Moreover, the United States is not the theocracy that Ireland is. There is a clear division between church and state, and American culture is infused with a more secular spirit. Religious belief ranges from the devout to the agnostic.

Brooklyn brings together Catholics from all over the world, each with their own subtle readings of Catholicism. In fact, according to Mrs Kehoe, Father Flood seems to have become more like the Italian priests in his manner. Intermarriage between individuals from different backgrounds – such as Diana Montini's parents or Tony and Eilis – will affect their perceptions of religion. Children from these unions will, in turn, inherit a fusion of Irish and Italian Catholicism, where the rigidity of the former is tempered by the greater tolerance of the latter. While the Italian faith is no less devout than Irish Catholicism, it is neither as judgemental nor as punitive. Furthermore, if individuals marry outside the Church – an impossible prospect in Ireland itself – the influence of Irish Catholicism would be muted to an even greater degree.

The impact of immigrating to America on Eilis' faith is implicit rather than explicit. There is no mention, for example, of her going to mass in Brooklyn; in a novel where details abound, this is an interesting omission. Certainly, after Rose's death Eilis finds no consolation in the spiritual, and the customary responses elude her. Eilis finds it impossible to think of Rose being 'up in heaven' (p.174), as the Catholic faith emphasises. Instead, it is the temporal rituals associated with death that preoccupy her. She says to Tony, 'I'll have to stop thinking about her dying and her coffin and all that and maybe start praying, but it's hard' (p.178). Rose's final incarceration, 'surrounded by darkness', is 'almost impossible to bear' (p.209), and Eilis feels 'gnawing sadness, almost guilt' (p.243) at her inability to pray as she believes she should.

Eilis' choice to sleep with Tony is noteworthy, given her Catholic faith. As well as furthering her relationship with him, it also says something about her willingness to take risks and empower herself. For Eilis the concept of sin is very real, and Catholic teaching unequivocally disapproves of sex before marriage. After she has had intercourse with Tony, Eilis' first instinct is to go to confession, and her immediate concern is pregnancy.

However, once she discovers that she is not pregnant, 'she thought of the night with pleasure' (p.191).

Perhaps it is being away from home, or the lack of attendant parental scrutiny, but for an Irish Catholic girl of the 1950s, the absence of residual guilt is startling. It suggests that Eilis is more subversive or less indoctrinated than most in her position. The situation is tacitly endorsed by the pragmatic response of the Italian priest who hears her confession. He 'somehow managed to imply that what had happened between her and Tony was not hard to understand ... and was maybe a sign from God that they should consider getting married and raising a family' (p.191). Had the same thing happened in Ireland, Eilis would have received greater condemnation.

Although the text acknowledges the central place of Catholicism in the lives of Irish immigrants, it also suggests that the power of the Irish Church may be offset by exposure to other cultural values. When these migrants interact with people whose Catholic upbringing has not determined their entire world view, the effect is significant.

QUESTIONS & ANSWERS

This section focuses on your own analytical writing on the text, and gives you strategies for producing high-quality responses in your coursework and exam essays.

Essay writing – an overview

An essay on a literary work is a formal and serious piece of writing that presents your point of view on the text, usually in response to a given topic. Your 'point of view' in an essay is your interpretation of the meaning of the text's language, structure, characters, situations and events, supported by detailed analysis of textual evidence.

Analyse – don't summarise

In your essays it is important to avoid simply summarising what happens in a text.

- A **summary** is a description or paraphrase (retelling in different words) of the characters and events. For example: 'Macbeth has a horrifying vision of a dagger dripping with blood before he goes to murder King Duncan.'
- An **analysis** is an explanation of the real meaning or significance that lies 'beneath' the text's words (and images, for a film). For example: 'Macbeth's vision of a bloody dagger shows how deeply uneasy he is about the violent act he is contemplating – as well as his sense that supernatural forces are impelling him to act.'

A limited amount of summary is sometimes necessary to let your reader know which part of the text you wish to discuss. However, always keep this to a minimum and follow it immediately with your analysis of what this part of the text is really telling us.

Plan your essay

Carefully plan your essay so that you have a clear idea of what you are going to say. The plan ensures that your ideas flow logically, that your argument remains consistent and that you stay on the topic. An essay plan should be a list of **brief dot points** – no more than half a page.

- Include your central argument or main contention – a concise statement (usually in a single sentence) of your overall response to the topic. See 'Analysing a sample topic' for guidelines on how to formulate a main contention.
- Write three or four dot points for each paragraph indicating the main idea and evidence/examples from the text. Note that in your essay you will need to *expand* on these points and *analyse* the evidence.

Structure your essay

An essay is a complete, self-contained piece of writing. It has a clear beginning (the introduction), middle (several body paragraphs) and end (the last paragraph or conclusion). It must also have a central argument that runs throughout, linking each paragraph to form a coherent whole.

See examples of introductions and conclusions in the 'Analysing a sample topic' and 'Sample answer' sections.

The introduction establishes your overall response to the topic. It includes your main contention and outlines the main evidence you will refer to in the course of the essay. Write your introduction *after* you have done a plan and *before* you write the rest of the essay.

The body paragraphs argue your case – they present evidence from the text and explain how this evidence supports your argument. Each body paragraph needs:

- **a strong topic sentence** (usually the first sentence) that states the main point being made in the paragraph
- **evidence** from the text, including some brief quotations
- **analysis** of the textual evidence explaining its significance and **explanation** of how it supports your argument
- **links back to the topic** in one or more statements, usually towards the end of the paragraph.

Connect the body paragraphs so that your discussion flows smoothly. Use some linking words and phrases like 'similarly' and 'on the other hand', though don't start every paragraph like this. Another strategy is to use a significant word from the last sentence of one paragraph in the first sentence of the next.

Use key terms from the topic – or synonyms for them – throughout, so the relevance of your discussion to the topic is always clear.

The conclusion ties everything together and finishes the essay. It includes strong statements that emphasise your central argument and provide a clear response to the topic.

Avoid simply restating the points made earlier in the essay – this will end on a very flat note and imply that you have run out of ideas and vocabulary. The conclusion is meant to be a logical extension of what you have written, not just a repetition or summary. Writing an effective conclusion can be a challenge. Try using these tips:

- Start by linking back to the final sentence of the second-last paragraph – this helps your writing to 'flow', rather than leaping back to your main contention straight away.
- Use synonyms and expressions with equivalent meanings to vary your vocabulary. This allows you to reinforce your line of argument without being repetitive.
- When planning your essay, think of one or two broad statements or observations about the text's wider meaning. These should be related to the topic and your overall argument. Keep them for the conclusion, since they will give you something 'new' to say but still follow logically from your discussion. The introduction will be focused on the topic, but the conclusion can present a wider view of the text.

Essay topics

1. 'Nothing can replace the loss of one's home.' Discuss.
2. 'Eilis Lacey is an unlikely heroine.' How does Tóibín show Eilis to be equal to the challenges presented to her?
3. 'This text shows that duty is more important than love.' Discuss.
4. "It was better to say yes than no." 'Eilis' biggest weakness is her desire to please.' Do you agree?
5. '*Brooklyn* demonstrates the selfish nature of love.' Discuss.
6. 'In immigrating to America, Eilis gains more than she loses.' Do you agree?
7. How is Catholicism shown to be a powerful force in the lives of the characters in *Brooklyn*?
8. "Brooklyn changes every day." How does Tóibín convey a sense of time and place in this novel?
9. 'Eilis will always feel like an outsider in America.' Discuss.
10. 'In *Brooklyn*, it is the men who are the decision-makers.' Do you agree?

Vocabulary for writing on *Brooklyn*

Irish Catholicism: the national religion of Ireland.

Linear structure: the structure of a narrative which presents events in chronological order.

Mass: the Catholic religious service that celebrates the Eucharist (the sacrament that commemorates the Last Supper with consecrated bread and wine).

Motif: a recurring image used to link ideas and reinforce themes; adds cohesion and unity to the writing.

Patriarchy: a society in which all of the power structures – political, religious, legal and domestic – are invested in men.

Rite of passage: a key event or experience in the growth and maturation of a young person.

Romance: a narrative that explores a romantic relationship between individuals.

Theocracy: a form of government in which there is a fusion of church and state.

Third-person limited: a form of narration in which the narrative point of view is limited to one character's perspective. That character is referred to as 'he' or 'she', but becomes the one with whom the reader most strongly identifies.

Sacraments: religious rites that are practised by Roman Catholics and believed to confer a state of grace on the recipients; for example, baptism, the Eucharist (mass and communion) and penance (confession).

Analysing a sample topic

"It was better to say yes than no." 'Eilis' biggest weakness is her desire to please.' Do you agree?

This question focuses on a particular aspect of Eilis' character and invites you to evaluate her behaviour. There are two or three assumptions here and you do not have to take any at face value. *Is* Eilis eager to please? *Is* this a weakness? If so, is it her *biggest* weakness? Make your contention clear in the introduction and indicate your line of argument.

- Examine Eilis' important relationships – with her family, with Tony and with Jim. To what extent does she try to please them?
- Would you describe her relationships at Bartocci's and Mrs Kehoe's boarding house in the same way? Does she always seek to please others in both places?
- Consider Eilis' motives. What lies behind her compliance? Is it love, loyalty, insecurity, fear or apathy? Are her choices positively or negatively driven?

- Most importantly, examine the consequences that flow from Eilis' behaviour. To what extent does she compromise her honesty and sense of self in trying to please others? Are they hurt by her actions?
- Do not overlook the fact that Eilis changes throughout the course of the novel. Is it reasonable to generalise in terms of her character?
- Acknowledge the context in which the quotation appears. What does this suggest about Mrs Lacey's influence and the values that Eilis has grown up with?
- It is also important to note the social context in which Eilis' story plays out. How much pressure was on young women to conform in the 1950s?

The following plan is *one* way to tackle the topic. While the weight of evidence in the text indicates that Eilis' desire to please *is* a problem, you could also present a more qualified argument.

Sample introduction

> Eilis Lacey does try hard to please others. Quiet and unassuming, it is not in her nature to oppose those she loves and, as a submissive youngest child, she is used to taking direction from her elders. When she has to operate independently, she often lacks the confidence and experience to act decisively in her own interests. Although Eilis learns to be more assertive in Brooklyn, her important choices are still driven by the needs and wishes of those around her. The fact that this leads to serious errors of judgement is evident with her family and, in particular, the two men in her life. Eilis is compromised and others are hurt by her misguided desire to please. In this sense, it is her biggest weakness.

Body paragraph outline

Paragraph 1: Temperament and conditioning have encouraged Eilis' compliance with regard to those she cares for.

- Eilis is obedient and self-effacing by nature.
- She is the youngest of five children.

- Eilis lives in a conservative society that is predicated on the submission of women.
- She is also educated in Christian values that encourage self-sacrifice: '"Of course I would, Mrs Kehoe" ... It was something her mother had taught her to say ...' (p.122).
- Note the way in which the quotation in the topic encapsulates her mother's philosophy.

Paragraph 2: Eilis defers to her mother and older sister, Rose.

- The decision to immigrate to America is imposed on Eilis by Rose, with practical support from Father Flood.
- Eilis has no say in where she lives or where she will work.
- Despite her unwillingness to leave home, she recognises her family's sacrifice and wishes to please them.
- She tells them little of her life in Brooklyn because she wants to protect her mother.
- In suppressing her own desires, she pays the cost in terms of homesickness, dislocation and the loss of close relationships with her family.

Paragraph 3: Eilis compromises herself in her relationships with Tony and Jim.

- Eilis allows Tony to rush her into marriage to alleviate his fear of losing her.
- She ignores her own reservations: 'I would like to marry him ... but I am not ready to marry him now' (p.190).
- Eilis loses opportunities regarding work and romance that are offered to her when she returns home to Enniscorthy.
- She is too ready to be what Jim wants her to be. She encourages his interest and avoids telling him the truth.
- Eilis behaves unfairly to Tony and Jim, and runs the risk of hurting them both.

Sample conclusion

Brooklyn demonstrates the importance of being true to oneself, showing that it is not necessarily 'better to say yes than no'. Although Eilis' actions are usually informed by generosity, and her intentions are worthwhile, ironically they can also result in hurting the very people she is trying to protect. In her dealings with those she cares about, her passivity and lack of conviction lead to significant mistakes. She seems reluctant to ask herself what *she* wants and to act on this knowledge. Conforming to the emotional demands of others must be seen as a weakness when the result is compromising or damaging.

SAMPLE ANSWER

'In this text, it is the men who are the decision-makers.' Do you agree?

Colm Tóibín's sensitive coming-of-age novel, *Brooklyn*, is set in Ireland and America in the early 1950s. It is a socially conservative time when women's choices are comparatively limited, as are their educational and professional opportunities. The majority of role models in authority are men. Ireland, in particular, is a patriarchal society, dominated by an uncompromising religious ethos and traditional gender expectations. However, while the broader social context may be unsympathetic to women as decision-makers, the text does present strong, proficient female characters who can, and do, make important decisions. This occurs in both a personal and professional capacity.

Women are shown to be independent and influential in the workplace. Elisabetta Bartocci is the driving force behind her father's business. As the public 'face' of Bartocci's, she conducts the initial interview with Eilis and makes her expectations with regard to the customers clear: 'You give them a big Irish smile.' The policies Miss Bartocci promotes are liberal. Generous incentives are offered to the store's mostly female workforce, encouraging women to further their qualifications and therefore improve their financial options. The decision to be the first retail business on the street to open its doors to black customers is both radical and bold. Miss Bartocci is clearly undeterred by the anticipated criticism, and the staff are instructed to 'be polite to anyone who comes into this store, coloured or white'. In Enniscorthy, Miss Kelly also runs her own establishment – a successful grocery store that sells 'the freshest of everything' in town. Having inherited the business from her parents, she is not answerable to anyone and manages the shop with autocratic precision.

Rose Lacey is, without doubt, the decision-maker in the Lacey family. Admittedly, her aberrant role has come about by default – it is only in the absence of her father and brothers that she has assumed responsibility for the welfare of her widowed mother and younger sister. Nevertheless, it is her income that supports them and, as such, she enjoys unchallenged authority within the family. Her approval is considered critical to any given enterprise. For example, when Eilis starts working at Miss Kelly's, Rose's ambivalence is a concern to both Eilis and her mother. Rose initiates and manages Eilis' immigration to the United States; this is in spite of Mrs Lacey's prior opposition to her daughter moving to England. Events are taken out of Eilis' – and, to a certain extent, Mrs Lacey's – hands, as Eilis' new life is organised by her older sister: 'Father Flood ... had been invited to the house because Rose knew that he could arrange it.'

The control these women have comes with a caveat – significantly, they are all unmarried. Society has required them to make a choice, and the likelihood of combining a career and motherhood is remote: 'In Bartocci's [Eilis] did not think any of the women in the office were married.' Eilis has neither Rose's assurance nor her social position, though it is no accident that on those occasions when she does act more decisively – with Mrs Kehoe and Father Flood – she is channelling her sister. Eilis' married life will bring constraints, particularly with regard to using her qualifications and pursuing an independent career. Yet, given the respect that Tony has for his wife and his desire to please her, it is likely that she will be a valued partner in decisions that affect their mutual future. Moreover, America has fuelled Eilis' ambitions, and her adaptability suggests that she will create opportunities for herself. Despite the societal expectation that she give up work after marriage, there is the possibility of involvement in the Fiorello business as a bookkeeper.

The roles assumed by the men in the text reflect the systemic discrimination that women suffer. Mr Bartocci is still the patriarch of his family business. At Brooklyn College, the majority of the students are male, as are the lecturers. Eilis' attendance is engineered by Father Flood, and the Jewish principal – also male – makes the decision to accept her. In addition, it would be disingenuous to discount the 'power of the collar' in the lives of these Irish characters, and the way in which the Catholic Church influences the decisions that women are allowed to make. Church leaders have decided on a moral code that committed Catholics, such as Eilis, feel bound by: 'they would both have to go to confession the following evening'. There is no doubt that Father Flood's endorsement of Rose's scheme helps to persuade the reluctant Mrs Lacey and adds credibility to the idea of Eilis' emigration.

The time and place in which the novel is set means that women do have limitations imposed on them by men. In general, conservative cultural and religious values deny women social equality. Most women, therefore, are not in a position to make or participate in key decisions. At the same time, *Brooklyn* demonstrates that it is certainly possible for individual women to assert themselves and act as decision-makers. In the foreground of his narrative, Tóibín has depicted strong, capable women who exercise substantial autonomy. Consequently, in this text, making decisions is not the exclusive prerogative of men.

REFERENCES & READING

Text

Tóibín, Colm 2009, *Brooklyn*, Penguin, London.

Websites

Colm Tóibín's official website: www.colmtoibin.com

Baines, Elizabeth 2010, 'Reading group: Brooklyn by Colm Toibin', 16 May, elizabethbaines.blogspot.com.au/2010/05/reading-group-brooklyn-by-colm-toibin.html

Hanks, Robert 2009, 'Brooklyn by Colm Tóibín: review', *The Telegraph*, 7 May, www.telegraph.co.uk/culture/books/bookreviews/5291609/Brooklyn-by-Colm-Toibin-review.html

Knox, Malcolm 2010, 'The Interview: Colm Toibin', *The Sydney Morning Herald*, 15 May, www.smh.com.au/entertainment/books/the-interview-colm-toibin-20100514-v3m4.html

McIlvanney, Liam 2009, 'The Coldest Place on Earth', *London Review of Books*, vol. 31, no. 12, June, www.lrb.co.uk/v31/n12/liam-mcilvanney/the-coldest-place-on-earth

Morton, Paul 2009, 'An Interview with Colm Toibin', June, www.bookslut.com/features/2009_06_014545.php

Schillinger, Liesl 2009, 'The Reluctant Emigrant', *The New York Times*, 1 May, www.nytimes.com/2009/05/03/books/review/Schillinger-t.html?pagewanted=all&_r=0

Tayler, Christopher 2009, 'The Country Girl', *The Guardian*, 9 May, www.guardian.co.uk/books/2009/may/09/colm-toibin-brooklyn

Yardley, Jonathan 2009, 'Book Review: "Brooklyn" by Colm Toibin', *The Washington Post*, 24 May, www.washingtonpost.com/wp-dyn/content/article/2009/05/22/AR2009052201123.html

Further reading

Barry, Sebastian 2011, *On Canaan's Side*, Faber, London.

Keogh, O'Shea and Quinlan (eds) 2004, *The Lost Decade: Ireland in the 1950s*, Mercier Press, Cork.

Tóibín, Colm 1992, *The Heather Blazing*, Picador, London.